LOVE LETTERS
FROM MOM
ON WHAT MATTERS MOST

To John, Julie, and Kevin
Never lose sight of your destiny!

Contents

Introduction

"You'll need a coat this morning—it's cold outside."
"Good luck on your test!"
"Drive carefully!"
"*Please* make your bed and pick up your room sometime today."
"How late is practice tonight? Will you be home for dinner?"
"I'll save you a plate."
"I love you. Have a great day."

In the blink of an eye, our children are gone—off to high school, their first job, then off to college. As moms, we hope that they become responsible, competent, strong, holy young adults. We also pray that they will have the self-confidence, common sense, and moral values to withstand the never-ending pressures of sex, drugs, and alcohol at every turn. But is that it? Do we simply want our teenagers to avoid the big pitfalls in life, and if they make it through college without too many battle scars, then we can breathe a sigh of relief and count our lucky stars? *No way!* There is so much we want to say, and so much more we want to impart as our children take wing and fly on their own. But too often, we are reluctant to say anything for fear of lecturing too much, nagging too often, or—Heaven forbid—becoming overbearing. And so, we retreat and say far too little about what matters most in life. Instead, we just repeat one of our standard parenting lines every morning as they head out the door, "I love you—have a great day." How can we be sure that the important life lessons don't get lost amid the countless verbal reminders or conversations that go in one ear and out the other? What can we do to "be there" for our young adult children when we can't physically reach them? And how can we possibly convey how much we love them?

I am writing this book because of something my dad did a long time ago to convey such love to me and impart wisdom. He did it only once in my life, but its impact was greater than he will ever know, and his message stuck. He wrote me a letter on May 6, 1983, the night of my Senior Prom:

Dear Patty,

Tonight should be a great night for you. I hope it is. You have had a terrific four years at Aquinas (High School), and we are very proud and happy for you. It would be a shame to have four fine years be ruined by a single night that did not turn out as you would like it to.

Remember, always use your head, and do what you decide is best, not what the crowd thinks is best.

Greg, I do not know you well enough to say whether you think for yourself or "go along with the crowd." But, judging by the fact you are taking my daughter

LOVE LETTERS
FROM MOM
ON WHAT MATTERS MOST

♡ Mom

PATTY SCHNEIER

**Chrysostom
Catholic Media**

to the Prom, I can only conclude you have excellent
taste and (are) quite a bit on the ball.

If there is any drinking problem please, don't drive.
Call me–I'll get you both home ... provided it is not
later than 11:30 p.m.!

Have a great time, Enjoy.
Dad

I have saved that letter for almost thirty years. It is one of my most treasured possessions because on that day, my dad revealed in his own special way what was in his heart: "I love you. You are precious to me. I am proud of you. Don't follow the crowd. Don't do anything you might regret." Had he spoken these words, they would have long since been forgotten. Instead, he wrote them down, and I could go back and re-read his precious love letter whenever I wanted. His letter meant a lot to me back in 1983, but it means so much more to me now. I have savored his golden words and re-read them many times throughout my adult life.

When I first became a parent, I followed in my father's footsteps and chose writing to reveal what was in my heart. For each of my children, I chose a special journal and wrote simple letters to capture the specific details of their life, record funny expressions, and recall how precious they were at age two, three, or four. I continued writing letters as they progressed through grade school and then high school, for I was still in awe of their growth and realized how quickly these childhood years were passing. Hopes, dreams, joys, sorrows, achievements, and special events from the tapestry of their life were all included. Finally, when they reached their sixteenth birthday, I gave them each their own completed, handwritten journal—sixteen years in the making, with every letter signed:

♡ Mom

One would think, "That should be enough." A journal filled with countless letters to each of my children should be *more* than enough! But it isn't. This is different. My children are now young adults, and there are many more important topics to be discussed that are crucial for their future—serious topics that require reflection, maturity, and an "openness" to hear. And so, once again I turn to writing to convey truth, to reveal my heart, and to hopefully impart lasting wisdom. I write in the best way I know how—love letters.

Love Letters from Mom, written in my own "maternal voice" with real stories about real people, is a compilation of letters to John, Julie, and Kevin Schneier. I dedicate this book to them, for if I die tomorrow, I want my children to have this as a physical, tangible remembrance of my love and gratitude. I want them to know what matters most, the purpose of life, the meaning of love, and what brings true joy as well. If no one else ever reads this book, that's okay. I feel compelled to write by God—often at 3:00 in the morning with a burning fire from within—and that is reason enough.

This book is also written for all of you mothers who are fellow sisters in Christ and comrades on this parenting journey. As the saying goes, "Once a mother, always a mother!" It doesn't matter if your son or daughter is ten, twenty, or forty years old; it doesn't matter if you have one child or twelve children. You and I are bonded in our desire to want what is best for our children and to be the best mother we can be. You and I both struggle to "reach" our teens as they mature and make decisions on their own, and often our hearts are pierced as our young adult children suffer the consequences of sin. What can we do? What can we say? How can we prevent them from abandoning the Catholic faith? How can we communicate truth in a way that they will receive it? These questions are as real for me as they are for you because I am no expert, nor do I have any foolproof answers. Still in the thick of parenting, the jury is still out regarding my own three children. But I do believe that if children experienced just half of what is in a mother's heart, they would melt.

We must convey with love and strength *why* we do the things we do, why we care about certain values, and why we must fight with every fiber of our being for their souls in this world. By sharing these personal letters with you, I hope to give you the confidence to share your heart with your children—without nagging or condemning—but with sound reasoning, practical examples, and encouragement. Do not be afraid to reveal your highest aims of truth, beauty, and love—for they resonate in the human heart. Perhaps after reading this book, you will give it to your teenager, college student, adult child, or grandchildren and simply say, "This is everything I want to say to you." Better yet, you will write a love letter to your children in your own words. Who knows? They might just keep it and treasure it forever!

Patty Schneier
September 23, 2011
Feast of St. Pio of Pietrelcina (Padre Pio)

Chapter 1

God Loves You—and so do I

"For God so loved the world that He gave His only Son, that whoever believes in Him should not perish but have eternal life."
(John 3:16)

Dear John, Julie, and Kevin,

I love you. I have loved each of you long before you were ever born, waiting for your arrival with joyful anticipation and hope for your future. Giving birth to you is by far the greatest accomplishment of my entire life, and I enjoy being your mother far more than you will ever know. You are a precious gift, and you are worth every sleepless night spent in a rocking chair, every trip to the doctor, every load of laundry, and every meal I have ever cooked for you. I love knowing you—sometimes better than you know yourself; I love watching you grow up to become all that you can be and cheering for you with every milestone you achieve. The joys of watching you take your first steps, ride a bike, open a Christmas present, play catch in the back yard, or dance on a stage are some of my most treasured memories. And yet, you are a source of joy—not only for your accomplishments—but simply for who you are as a unique, irreplaceable member of our family. As my child, your dreams are my dreams, your goals become my goals, and your sufferings cause my heart to break.

John's first steps   Julie's first dance recital   Kevin's first tricycle

I love you with a love that will never end—*never*. No matter what the future holds, no matter what you choose to do with your life, or where you choose to live, I will always love you with a deep maternal love. Even if your mind fails or your body ceases to move, I will love you. I will love you through the painful failures, broken hearts, and tragic losses that are bound to come your way. I will love you when you don't necessarily love me in return, when I must love you from a distance, or when you don't love yourself. There might be times when I will remain silent or seem indifferent, but I will still love and care for you. At other times, I will strongly disagree and argue with you—often with every ounce of my being—because I love you so much and only want what is best for you. You are worth the fight. In the end, however, I will love you enough to let you go your own way. Ultimately, you do not belong to me. You never have. You were given to me as a gift here on earth, to nurture and care for, to teach and to love for a very short time. But you are destined to experience perfect love for all eternity with the One who created you. You are meant to participate in the eternal exchange of love between the Father, Son, and Holy Spirit—which is a love we cannot even fathom!

As much as I love you and want what is best for you, God loves you infinitely more than I do. My imperfect, human love pales in comparison to the love God has for you since the beginning of time, which continues for all eternity. His love is personal and passionate. He knows every hair on your head, every thought in your brain, and every move you make. You are the apple of His eye, the crown of His creation. He delights in you. You are His precious child. He lavishes His love every day upon you. Just look at the stars, listen to the ocean, stare at a flower, or watch the sunset. He surrounds you with beauty and the wonder of creation simply because He loves you; He created this world out of nothing and created you and me simply out of love.

And then, God showed us the greatest love of all. God could have looked down on the world, seen all its brokenness, and destroyed the world in an instant. He could have thought, "Bad experiment! What a waste of my gifts!" But He didn't. While we were sinners, God entered into our misery. He entered the messiness of humanity, even if it meant suffering and dying in order to save us from ourselves. And so, God took on our very nature, and the Second Person of the Trinity became man. *And the Word became flesh and dwelt among us. (John 1:14)* Jesus Christ, Emmanuel, is God's ultimate act of love for you and me. This is the foundation of Christianity—that God would become a man. It is so radical. No other religion on the planet reveals a God who loves us so much that He becomes human, is born of a woman, suffers, dies, and rises from the dead to save us! And yet, the name *Emmanuel* literally means "God with us." God wants to be with us at every moment and to love us with a love so powerful that it overcomes sin, loneliness, violence—even death itself. The greatest gift that God could ever give us is His own Son, Jesus, who came to reveal the Father's love and show us how to love.

Today, more than ever, our world is searching for true love. I try to love in a million different ways, but often fail. John, remember when I completely overreacted and yelled at you for getting a "C" on your first test in high school? I failed to love on that day. You try to love and fail sometimes as well. We don't know how to love the very people who are closest to us. Nations don't know how to love one another and live in peace. Families are broken, lives are shattered, violence rages on. In the midst of this, Jesus invites you and me to receive His love and then be transformed by this love. *Love one another as I have loved you. (John 15:12)* How can we do that? How can we experience the love of God that is more powerful than sin, able to heal broken hearts, and triumph over suffering? How can we know what this love looks like? Does it even exist in our world today? I believe it does, but you have to know where to look. Look to Jesus Himself. His entire life reveals what true love really is.

I want you to experience the love of God found in Christ Jesus. It can make all the difference in your life. I pray you will receive this love as a free gift from your Heavenly Father who is madly, passionately in love with you. I also hope you will let it transform your heart and change your life so that you can love God and others in return. My own world changed drastically at age thirty-six when I was introduced to the writings of Christopher West and Pope John Paul II's *Theology of the Body*. It was then that I finally learned how to articulate one of the most mysterious words in the universe—love. Real love, exemplified by Christ, is always *free, faithful, total, and fruitful.* These four words gave me a totally new understanding and appreciation for God's unconditional love and how we are to love others. I want you, along with the whole world, to know and understand this awesome love!

First and foremost, God's love is always a *freely* given gift. Jesus revealed this aspect of love when He freely chose to suffer and die. He could have come down from the Cross, but He didn't. He freely gave his life for you and for me, surrendering His own Will to save mankind. It was a pure gift with no strings attached because love doesn't manipulate, coerce, or grasp at another. Simply stated, you can't force authentic friendship or love. It must be mutually given and received in total freedom. Think of adoption, an organ transplant, or a blood donation to save a life. When freely given and freely received, these are beautiful gifts of authentic love.

Secondly, God's love is *faithful.* Jesus didn't love us just for six weeks. He loved us until death. He loved those who spit upon Him, whipped Him, tortured Him, and pounded nails in His hands and feet. He loved His disciples when they abandoned Him. Moreover, Jesus promised to be with us *until the end of the age. (Matthew 28:20)* Real love never quits—even in the worst of circumstances—and never dies—even beyond the grave. Look to your own two sets of grandparents who have both been married for over fifty years. Their love has persevered through the trials of cancer, unemployment, dementia, and the loss of a son and son-in-law. That's faithful love. That's the real deal.

Also, God's love is *total.* Jesus didn't say, "You can nail me to the Cross, but don't put the nails in my feet." He didn't say, "You can have all of me, just not my hands." No. When Jesus was crucified on that Cross, it was His whole body that was crucified, a total gift of self. Every last drop of blood was shed for you and for me. He held nothing back. This is real love. That's why a mother's love is so special. She literally surrenders her body for nine months to carry the life within her. Then, she lays down her body again through the shedding of blood, sweat, and tears to give life to her child. Trust me—it's a total gift of self!

Finally, God's love is *fruitful* and life-giving. It is not stagnate or sterile. He came that we might *have life and have it to the full. (John 10:10)* The Father pours out His love to the Son who receives it, and the fruit of this love is the Holy Spirit. Likewise, you are the very fruit of the love I have for your father. He pours out his love for me, I receive the gift of his love, and new life is conceived within me. You are that beautiful, tangible, eternal fruit of our marriage. If I have never told you in person, let me tell you now: You are not a liability. You are not a burden. You are the beautiful fruit of our love that will last for all eternity, and when I look at you, I am in awe of this miracle.

Free, faithful, total, and fruitful—it all sounds so awesome, and it is. But there is something that binds these all together, and you must recognize it in order to fully understand the true nature of love. Free, faithful, total, and fruitful love is lived out in the context of sacrifice. Once again, it is Jesus who gives us the perfect example. Jesus exemplified the sacrificial nature of love when He took upon Himself all the sin and suffering of humanity on the Cross. If you simply stare at a crucifix long enough, ponder the Stations of the Cross, or watch the movie, *The Passion of the Christ,* it becomes unmistakable. Love hurts. Love costs. Love demands our very life. That's the message of the Cross, and sometimes, the Cross can weigh heavily on our heart. Fortunately, that is not the end of the story, however! The power of God's love in the Resurrection transforms suffering and sacrifice into victory and joy. It sounds crazy, but it's true. Real love transcends pain and even death.

What could possibly make Mother Teresa move to Calcutta to work in the streets with the poorest of the poor and the dying? What could make St. Maximilian Kolbe freely offer to go to the starvation bunker in Auschwitz in place of another man and suffer a torturous death? Why does your grandmother sit in a nursing home day after day, hour after hour with your grandfather, who may or may not even know who she is on any given day? And why did Jesus submit Himself to Roman scourging and crucifixion? There's only one way to explain it. He wanted to do it. It had to be love. And for Mother Teresa, St. Maximilian Kolbe, or your grandmother, the reason is the same. For any parent who has ever held vigil at the bedside of a sick child or worked a second job to make ends meet, the reason is the same as well. Love demands sacrifice, but the sacrifice is born willingly out of love. Nothing else matters. The sacrifice is worth it.

That's the kind of love I hope you experience in your life—love that is free, faithful, total, and fruitful—lived out in sacrifice and joy. The source is God, and only His love will satisfy the deepest desires of your heart. Fame, fortune, sex, power, and pleasure will never be enough because as St. Augustine so beautifully said, "You have made us for yourself, O Lord, and our hearts are restless until they rest in you." The question for your life is: Do you believe it? Do you believe in His personal, perfect love for you, manifested in Jesus? Do you believe that God's love is stronger than any disappointment, any tragedy, any sin, failure, sickness, or addiction? Do you believe it can melt the most hardened heart? No one else can answer these questions for you. I can try with all my heart to tell you about God's amazing love, surround you with His love, and hopefully give witness to His love. I can share story after story about the power of God's love working in my life and how His love sustains me at every moment. I would be lost without Him, no doubt about it, and I don't want to live one *second* without Him. What about you? Your answer determines your future.

If you experience difficulties in life or begin to doubt the existence of God, look at creation and remember how much God loves you—so much so that He created this world for you and was willing to die for you. Whenever I fail you as a parent, remember that God is your perfect, loving parent at all times. You are His. He has adopted you. You have a royal inheritance that awaits you! God loves you as the perfect Father, Creator, Friend, Savior, and Lover of your soul. He has a plan for your life, *plans for welfare and not for evil, to give you a future and a hope.* (*Jeremiah 29: 11*) His Will for you is love. His purpose is always love. You can trust Him with your life.

Remember, I love you so much, and I love being your mother. But far more important is for you to know of God's unconditional, personal, passionate love. Receive His love. Experience His love. Live in His love. It's the greatest romance, the greatest journey, and the greatest love story ever.

♡ *Mom*

November 11, 2011
Feast of St. Martin of Tours

Chapter 2

Sin—and why I want you to hate it

"If we say, 'We are without sin,' we deceive ourselves, and the truth is not in us."

(1 John 1:8)

Dear John, Julie, and Kevin,

I love you and think the world of you. You each have so many gifts and talents, excelling in sports, music, drama, and academics. As your mother, I am your biggest fan, and I am confident you will do great things with your life. People admire you for your hard work, your honesty, your fun-loving nature, and kindness to all. I am often told by coaches and teachers, "Your son is awesome! Your daughter is amazing! You have one great kid." In all of these cases, they are not referring to your report card or talents, but to your character. I swell with pride and can't help but agree. I'm the luckiest mom in the world. You are a role model for other teens; you give hope for the future. Each of you is a good and wonderful person.

Now, before you get a big head and pat yourself on the back, let me also tell each of you with complete honesty that you are a sinner. I know your sins, and they are many. I have seen you act selfishly, lose your temper, overreact, disobey, and lie about it. At times, you have treated others horribly, used foul language, and behaved like a complete jerk. Moreover, you can be moody, lazy, rude, and absolutely obnoxious. The truth is ... you have a dark side that you don't want other people to see because it isn't pretty. But then again, you could say the exact same thing about me because you know my sins as well as I know yours. You have seen *my* dark side and can attest, "It isn't pretty."

Sin: It's what we all have in common with every other person in the world, for *all have sinned and fall short of the glory of God. (Romans 3:23)* Literally, the word *sin* means to "miss the mark," as in archery when the arrow misses the target. When we sin, we freely choose something instead of God's love. We know it is wrong, but we choose it anyway. It doesn't mean we are a bad person, for usually behind every sin is a fear, an old wound, or an emptiness we are trying to fill—as in drug or alcohol abuse, addictive gambling, or spending. Often, we take something good, true, and beautiful—such as the human body and the gift of sexuality—and we distort it. We twist the meaning and purpose. We "miss the mark." God's love helps us to untwist the lies and distortions. It reminds us that we are made for something more and that ultimately, our deepest longings can only be fulfilled in Him.

Sin is always personal, but never private. There is a ripple effect to others, like throwing a rock in the water. No matter how large or small the rock may be, it will automatically cause a ripple. In the same way, sin affects our own self *and* others. There is always someone on the receiving end of my anger, revenge, or greed—usually someone I love. Sin is also our greatest personal tragedy because eventually it consumes and destroys us. It destroys our mind, our body, our relationships, our conscience, and our integrity. Sin always leads to suffering, pain, and chaos. Think of fire, for example. Fire is good for heating and cooking. Without fire, man would die in certain environments. In a home, a fire in the fireplace gives warmth and enjoyment to all. But take that fire out of the fireplace, and it will quickly consume the house, destroy it, injure innocent people, and cause death. In the same way, listen to the nightly news or read the daily headlines. Behind almost every tragic story, you will find sin that has consumed and destroyed God's beautiful gifts.

Do not be deceived. A small fire can quickly become a large fire. Venial sins can easily become mortal sins. We don't like to talk about it, but there is such a thing as mortal sin. Sins against the Ten Commandments fall into this category. With grave matter, full knowledge, and deliberate consent, you cut yourself off from the grace of God. Note: God does *not* cut you off. He is always there with love, mercy, and an open invitation. You cut yourself off by turning away from God, and He loves you so much that He gives you free will. He lets you go. He will not force you to accept His invitation because that is not love. Remember, love can never be forced. But if you stubbornly cling to mortal sin over God, you squander your inheritance by your own choosing. Mortal sin is death to the soul. *The Parable of the Prodigal Son* in Luke's Gospel illustrates this perfectly:

The prodigal son originally lived in harmony with his father, but he chose money and worldly pleasures over that relationship. He chose to leave and cut himself off from the family. The father did not stop him; he let his son go. Through a lifestyle of immorality, reckless spending, and wild partying, the son completely squandered his inheritance. It was gone. Had he never returned, he would have died in his own sin, in a faraway land, apart from his father. We do not know how long the father waited for his son to return home. It could have been weeks, months, years, or even decades. But throughout that time, however long and painful it must have been, the father did not go after his son nor force him to come home.

Notice what the father said when his son did repent and return: *Quick! Bring the best robe and put it on him. Put a ring on his finger and sandals on his feet. Bring the fattened calf and kill it. Let's have a feast and celebrate. For this son of mine was dead and is alive again; he was lost and is found. (Luke 15:22-24)* Why did the father say his son was *dead*, when we know full well he was still physically alive? The father is referring here to his spiritual life. The son had been living in a state of mortal sin. He had freely chosen to turn away from his father, and therefore, his soul was spiritually dead. This is a story that ended well, but only because the son finally came to his senses, had a conversion of heart, and returned home, where the father was waiting to restore his dignity and his inheritance. How many people do not come to their senses? How many die in a state of mortal sin, clinging to worldly pleasures and refusing to come home? They are spiritually dead.

Do not think, however, that mortal sin is committed only by those who are viciously evil or that venial sins do not matter in the scheme of things. They do. For example, if you simply say the following words: 9/11, Oklahoma City Bombing, Columbine High School, or Virginia Tech Massacre, most adults can vividly remember the horror and devastation of these events. But as a wise retreat master once told me, "We don't need to fly an airplane into a skyscraper to cause destruction. We do it every day with our own words and actions. You and I don't need a gun in our hand or a bomb in our car either." (Fr. Jim Burshek, S.J) We can destroy a person's reputation with one vulgar comment posted on a Facebook photo. We destroy a person's spirit with one cruel joke; we destroy another's confidence with one negative remark.

It's true. I have crushed you many times with my own harsh criticisms, unrealistic expectations, and false accusations—and I know it. I have offended people I love and lost friendships by my own carelessness, neglect, unsolicited suggestions, or my overbearing assertiveness. I can sling razor sharp words like arrows, "go for the jugular" to win any argument, and perfectly hit my target every time. This is the everyday, ordinary venial sin that destroys. But it, too, can affect people for the rest of their lives, and often we don't realize it.

Why are we so blind to our own sin, both venial and mortal? The answer is simple: We disregard sin in our culture. We refuse to acknowledge sin or call it by its proper name. The seven deadly sins of lust, gluttony, greed, sloth, wrath, envy, and pride are alive and well, but we don't often hear about these words, much less use them in our own vocabulary. It's easier to talk in terms of "faults" or "bad habits," "addictions" or "abuse," "epidemics" or "societal problems." Not many are willing to point out—for fear of being labeled "judgmental"—that the problems caused by pre-marital sex, sexually transmitted infections, sexual abuse, sexual assault, adultery, pornography, and masturbation are all the result of lust and its empty promises. Does anyone look at the obesity problem in our country and acknowledge that we are a gluttonous people? We are a nation of triple cheeseburgers, eating and drinking contests, and thirty-two-ounce sodas, yet no one dares to call over-eating sinful—but it is. The amount I eat on 4th of July, Christmas, and Thanksgiving is also gluttonous, but I often rationalize it by saying, "It's a holiday," and then I allow myself to go way overboard. It's sinful.

We are a people of greed when we buy more toys, more clothes, more shoes, and more gadgets than necessary. I admit, I buy too many shoes, own too many jackets, and greedily desire more money for vacations. But often, I just call these my "weaknesses." We are a people of sloth when we don't give an honest day's work for an honest day's pay or waste the day in front of the TV, surfing the internet, or playing video games. When we habitually don't pray, don't exercise, or don't study— and we know we should—it is sinful. It is sloth (laziness.) We commit the sin of wrath every time we seek revenge, hold a grudge, or refuse to forgive someone. We are a people of envy when we are never satisfied with our possessions or we compare ourselves to others.

Last but not least, there is pride—the deadliest sin of all and the foundation of all other sins. In choosing our own desires over God's commands, pride leads us to rationalize our actions, decide that we know best, and disobey. We are prideful when we desire attention, recognition, or prestige. Pride also causes us to worry about our own reputation and tell lies to cover up our faults and failings. I am guilty of lust, gluttony, greed, sloth, wrath, envy, and pride time and time again. You are, too. But as an old Chinese proverb says, "The first step in wisdom is to call things by their proper name." It is important to call a spade a spade. Only then can healing and new life begin.

In my own life, I spent years driving over the speed limit and thought it was no big deal. I was a horrible driver, but simply excused this "little fault" of mine. Not until I received three tickets within eighteen months did I ever stop to think that my "little problem" was the result of sin. However, on January 6, 2009, as a police officer wrote me a ticket for speeding through a residential zone, I had an unexpected conversation with God in the silence of my heart. I remember thinking, "I have a problem here." I felt God whisper back, "No, you don't have a *problem* here—you have *sin* here." To which I replied, "Okay, God, show me my sin."

Immediately, I saw my habitual speeding in a whole new light. I was guilty of the sin of pride, arrogantly thinking I was above the law and didn't have to follow these minor rules. Pride caused me to ignore speed limits and do whatever it takes to be on time. When I thought about *why* I did this, I realized it was pride in my reputation. I worried about what people would think if I were late. Words like *impatience, disobedience,* and *selfish disregard for the safety of others* were suddenly staring at me in the face. Finally, I saw that I had made my schedule, my to-do list, and my daily agenda my false god to which I bowed every morning in my desire to accomplish my daily goals.

When I saw speeding in its true light and realized that I was "an accident waiting to happen," I despised the ugliness of my sin. I did not want to be the woman who carelessly ran over a young child or hit another car simply because I was in a hurry. I did not want to get another ticket, nor did I want the stress of slamming on my brakes every time I passed a police car, praying that the officer wouldn't pull me over. I did not want to be a hypocrite. And yet, I *was* a hypocrite every time I told you as a new driver to slow down and be careful. In that moment, I realized I had "missed the mark." I was not the person I wanted to be. Something was wrong, and that something was *sin*. Yet God, in His love, was giving me a wake-up call and an invitation. That speeding ticket was a gift. It made me long for Confession. I wanted to receive God's mercy and get rid of this sin once and for all.

I must continually ask God for the grace to recognize sin in my life because so often, I just don't see it. It is much easier to dig in my heels, insist I have done nothing wrong, or justify my minor faults. Now, I pray that simple prayer whenever I am frustrated, when things aren't right, or something is out of balance. "God, show me my sin." He answers every time. But that process of naming sin for what it is can be the most important step. Ultimately, our sins do not prevent us from achieving holiness. Rather, it is the stubborn *denial* of sin that prevents us from holiness. If you refuse to acknowledge sin in your life, you are bound to remain a slave to it. Name it. In doing so, you will acquire a "sense of sin." A "sense of sin" is simply an awareness of how much God loves you and how you have failed to respond to that love. Moreover, it's an awareness of who God is and who you are—and how *big* that gap is.

After witnessing a miraculous catch of fish, St. Peter felt this "sense of sin" and said, *"Depart from me, Lord, for I am a sinful man." (Luke 5:8)* And yet, Jesus had no problem handing Peter the keys to the Kingdom of Heaven, establishing His Church upon the rock of Peter, and choosing him to lead the Apostles. Why? Peter's sense of sin and recognition of his own weakness made Peter desire to follow Jesus. Peter knew he was in need of a Savior; he would rely on God. He would have compassion for other sinners as well. That was the beginning of his holiness. Even though he would sin again and deny that he knew Jesus, he still became a great saint because he was humble enough to recognize his sin, seek forgiveness, and be restored to Christ. He is a model for us to do the same. Name the sin, hate sin, repent of sin, but do not despair over sin.

There was one time in my life when I did despair over my sin, and it was awful. Thankfully, the despair did not last very long. After discovering the *Theology of the Body* and the beauty of God's free, faithful, total, and fruitful love, I recognized for the first time in my life that contraception was a counterfeit to authentic love. I wept for days when I realized we had settled for a counterfeit and had "missed the mark" in our marriage. I wept because I longed for truth and authentic love, but I didn't know how to get it. I wept for the realization that I had been a stubborn, "prodigal" child for thirteen years, and all the while, God had been patiently and lovingly waiting for me to turn around and see this. I wept out of shame, regret, and guilt—for the hypocrisy in my life as a Catholic who had dissented from the Church. I wept for the realization that I had received Holy Communion in a state of mortal sin for thirteen years and didn't think a thing of it.

The enormity of this was crushing. I was a mess, but I was too embarrassed to confess my secret sin, too embarrassed to tell a priest who saw me every Sunday, and too afraid to throw away the contraception once and for all. This was the worst week of my life. I was depressed and could barely function. I was robbed of all joy. Guilt and shame consumed me. Confession was the only remedy. (I'll write more about that later.) I am so grateful that the desire for unity—with God and with my husband—was *much* stronger than my despair. Do not despair over your sins. Turn to God, and *though your sins are like scarlet, they shall be as white as snow. (Isaiah 1:18)*

Now, when I look back, I am also grateful that I wept. Though it was horrible at the time, my tears were necessary. They led me to true repentance and helped me to see that I was no different than Peter when he denied Jesus. After hearing the rooster crow three times, Peter *went outside and wept bitterly. (Matthew 26:75)* Yes, it is good to weep for our sins. I have learned this from parenting you. If you completely blow it, but come back to me with tears in your eyes and say you are sorry, I cannot help but forgive you. When your tears are sincere, they are beautiful, and I end up crying too. In the same way, I have seen countless women with tears in their eyes approach me after giving a talk at a conference. I hug them. I tell them their tears are beautiful, and that God wants to turn their tears into dancing and joy. The same is true for you. Go ahead; it's okay. Weep for your sins. Your tears are beautiful. It is a sign that you realize how much God loves you, and how badly you "missed the mark."

One time, I sat alone in an empty church and wept for hours because of my sin. In February 2010, I was in Cold Lake, Alberta, where it was forty below zero outside. I had the entire day to myself before speaking that night at a parish, and I looked forward to spending the afternoon at the church in prayer. After about two hours, I decided to pray the Stations of the Cross, and when I came to the 11th Station, *Jesus is Crucified*, I stared at the image on the wall. Normally, I focus on Jesus whenever I ponder this scene and imagine the pain He endured while being nailed to the Cross.

However, on this day, I turned my attention to the Roman soldier. My eyes were fixed on him—with his hammer raised in the air and his hand ready to pound. I couldn't move. And I said to myself, "How could any human being do that to another? How could he inflict so much pain? Does he *realize* he is killing the Son of God? I would hate to be *that* guy." My next thought hit me like a ton of bricks, "Patty, you *are* that guy." Suddenly, I could recall events in my life when I had hurt someone. Some of these memories had been repressed for years, and I had never given them a second thought. Recalling them was painful.

And then, this question blindsided me, "Lord, how many times have I caused pain and suffering *and I'm not even aware of it?* A dozen times? Fifty times? One hundred times? How many times have I been the Roman soldier and was so oblivious that I don't remember?" That thought pierced me, and I wept for hours because of my sin. I will never forget that experience. Someday, it will hit you, too—like a ton of bricks—

that you are the Roman soldier. Weep for your sins, but do not despair. I love you, and God loves you even more.

One final thought: Beware of secrets. As a young adult, your secrets are far more serious than the little secrets from childhood. Secrets erode your conscience and demand effort to keep concealed. Often, they require lying or telling half-truths to maintain, and so begins a downward spiral of slavery which holds you in bondage. *Nothing is concealed that will not be revealed, nor secret that will not be known. (Matthew 10:26)* Only when secrets are brought to the light can true freedom and healing be restored.

Unfortunately, it took me a long time to learn this lesson. Your father and I kept the use of contraception a secret for thirteen years. The entire time, we were afraid that someone would see us purchase contraception at the store or that one of you would find a box of condoms in the bathroom. We went to great lengths—ridiculous lengths—to secretly purchase and hide them. Why did we go out of our way to keep this secret? Because we knew it was wrong. Shame is a warning signal, and we should have taken notice, but we didn't. Behind the secret was *sin*, and for thirteen years, we were not willing to give up the sin, so we worked hard to keep the secret. Beware of secrets. *As long as I kept silent, my bones wasted away; I groaned all the day. For day and night your hand was heavy upon me; my strength withered as in dry summer heat. Then I declared my sin to you; my guilt I did not hide. I said, "I confess my faults to the Lord," and you took away the guilt of my sin ... Many are the sorrows of the wicked, but love surrounds those who trust in the Lord. Be glad in the Lord and rejoice, you just; exult, all you upright of heart. (Psalm 32:3-5, 10-11)*

The bottom line is that you were made for union with God, to be with Him for all eternity. You were not made for sin. No sin is worth destroying yourself or others. God wants so much more for you, and so do I. Despise sin and avoid it at all cost. Name it, recognize it, and repent of it quickly when you fall. Remember, you can always come home. Just turn around, and God will be waiting for you with open arms. So will I.

I love you more than you can fathom—with all your sins, faults, and failings. Thank you for loving me despite my sinfulness as well.

♡ mom

November 16, 2011
Feast of St. Margaret of Scotland

Chapter 3

Heaven—and why I want you to be there

"But our citizenship is in Heaven, and from it we also await a Savior, the Lord Jesus Christ."
(Philippians 3:20)

Dear John, Julie, and Kevin,

It's November, one of my favorite months. Having just celebrated All Saints Day and the Feast of All Souls, the Church gives us this month to ponder the four last things: death, judgment, Heaven, and hell. This is not morbid or depressing, but rather a season of joy and hope. I love this time of year. I love reminiscing and feeling connected to my grandparents, relatives, and friends who have died. Also, it is good for us in our fast-paced lifestyle to stop once in a while and reflect on our destiny. Pondering death, judgment, Heaven, and hell is a healthy dose of reality, and as your mother, it is my job to prepare you for your future—your ultimate future.

The first reality of your future is death. Just as the leaves are falling outside, we will also return to the earth someday, for every living thing must die. No one escapes it. We do not get to choose the day, the hour, or how God will call us home. Although we all hope for a long and happy life for ourselves and those we love, there are no guarantees. Sometimes, death is sudden. Sometimes, after much suffering, it is long in coming. God, the Creator of Life, is in control of these details, and that mystery can be difficult for us to understand—no matter how old we are or how many deaths we have witnessed.

I am certainly no expert on death, but I have had the unique privilege of singing countless funerals and journeying closely with loved ones as they prepared for death. Also, I was at the side of your Uncle Tom, Uncle Mike, and my friend Mary when they breathed their last breath. What a sacred, intimate moment. Each of these unique experiences with death taught me so much. Mary was just forty years old with three young children when she was diagnosed with brain cancer. She shared with me her fears and asked many questions about death and Heaven. You may have similar questions. While I do not have any educated, theological answers, I can share with you an analogy that has helped me to understand and to trust God with the details of my own death. I understand death in terms of being born—the process of labor and delivery.

When you were born into this world, you had no choice in the matter whatsoever. You did not get to choose if your delivery would be long or short, two weeks early, or one month late. You did not get to choose if you would be delivered naturally with no medication, by C-section, breech, or with the help of forceps. And certainly, the process for you as a newborn was quite traumatic. You had to leave the comfort of the womb, where it was safe, quiet, and warm—where everything you needed was automatically given to you. You also experienced hours of intense contractions, screaming, pushing, and pulling to force you out into this world.

Then in those early days and weeks, you had to endure so many new sensations and experiences: nakedness, light, heat, cold, hunger, wetness, pain, and tears. You could not talk, walk, or change anything. You were completely helpless. Yet, throughout the process of delivery and in those first moments after birth, could you have ever dreamed what your life would be like and all the promise it would hold? Could you have ever known all that you would see, hear, touch, taste, smell, learn, and experience in this beautiful, awesome world? No. You couldn't fathom what awaited you. All you had previously known was life in the womb, but you were never meant to stay there. You were meant to be born and experience *this* life.

The process of your birth may have been traumatic, but you don't even remember it now. John, your delivery was horrible, and you arrived bruised and battered from suction and forceps. Julie, your delivery was crazy. We called our parents from the hospital at 10:00 p.m. and told them to go to bed; you probably wouldn't arrive until morning. Thirty minutes later, with no time for an epidural shot, you were born! I can still remember the nurses trying to grab the doctor, screaming in the hallway, "Get in here! She's made her move, and she's going fast!" Kevin, you were late. Everyone thought you would weigh ten pounds or more because I was so big. I simply could not wait for you to be born—no matter what it involved. To everyone's surprise, you weighed in at an even eight pounds. In the scheme of things, it doesn't matter if you were born after a long and grueling delivery or if it only took a few hours. All that matters is that you were born. Now, you can't fathom going back to life in the womb. That's how I view death. Death is like the unknown, traumatic process of labor and delivery. And just as we were never meant to stay in our mother's womb, we were never meant to stay here either—even though we can't fathom what awaits us.

Truly, it is the hope of Heaven and promise of salvation in Jesus Christ that takes the fear out of death. Jesus has conquered death; the victory has already been won! *Death is swallowed up in victory. Where, O death, is your victory? Where, O death, is your sting? (1 Corinthians 15:55)* I have witnessed firsthand that faith in this victory brings tremendous peace and strength at the moment of death. But we must not forget that judgment also awaits us, and a healthy dose of "fear of the Lord" is a good thing. Remember, God is a just Judge as well as a loving Father, and He shows no partiality. *Not everyone who says to me, "Lord, Lord," will enter the Kingdom of Heaven, but only the one who does the Will of my Father in Heaven. (Matthew 7:21)*

I don't claim to understand or be able to articulate the judgment of "the living and the dead," which we profess in the Creed every Sunday, but I do know this: You and I will be judged by our every word and action. Do not take judgment lightly. Over and over again, Scripture tells us that God *will repay everyone according to his works: eternal life to those who seek glory, honor, and immortality through perseverance in good works, but wrath and fury to those who selfishly disobey the truth and obey wickedness. (Romans 2:6-8)*

Also, *when the Son of Man comes in His glory, and all the angels with Him, He will sit upon His glorious throne, and all the nations will be assembled before Him. And He will separate them one from another, as a shepherd separates the sheep from the goats. He will place the sheep on His right and the goats on His left. Then the king will say to those on His right, "Come, you who are blessed by my Father. Inherit the Kingdom prepared for you from the foundation of the world. For I was hungry and you gave me food, I was thirsty and you gave me drink, a stranger and you welcomed me, naked and you clothed me, ill and you cared for me, in prison and you visited me."* *(Matthew 25:31-36)*

I want to be there! I hope for Heaven, live for Heaven, and trust in the promise of Heaven. I thank God that Christ has opened the gates of Heaven to all who believe in Him. By His Passion, Death, and Resurrection, He has made it possible for us to live with God in perfect union, total happiness, and endless beauty forever. This is true paradise! But I will not presume automatic, instant Heaven—nor should you. I am not perfect. I do not know how to love perfectly in all circumstances. This side of Heaven, I will still be flawed up to the moment of my death. For even though I confess my sins and God forgives me, I know that I sin again and again and again. Why do I do this when I am forgiven? The answer is simple: My tendency to sin remains.

God, who can do all things by His power, love, and mercy, is the only one who can make me perfect. He can purify my heart, purge me of any selfishness that remains, and remove my attachments to material goods. He can do whatever it takes so that I will be made perfect and capable of total union with Him. *Nothing unclean shall enter Heaven. (Revelation 21:27)* (Otherwise, it wouldn't be Heaven!) It would be absurd to presume that I will be perfect at the moment of my death. Nevertheless, God takes me as I am and loves me. So if He purifies me in an instant, an hour, a day, a week, a year, or a hundred years, it doesn't matter. Time is irrelevant in eternity. *But do not ignore this fact, beloved, that with the Lord one day is like a thousand years and a thousand years like one day. (2 Peter 3:8)*

Also, out of love and perfect justice, He can perfect my soul any way He chooses. If He wants my soul to be purified like gold in the furnace, then I will not refuse the flames of His love. I want any last remaining tendency of sin to be burned away. By His grace, the flames will lead me to His presence. This purification is Purgatory. It is not a place, not a waiting room for Heaven, nor a punishment for the damned. I am assured of salvation if I live and die in God's grace, and I praise God that He will purify me in order to experience the joys of Heaven. The result is glorious perfection forever, in union with the Lover of my soul and in the company of all the saints. That is my goal!

Then I saw a new Heaven and a new earth. The former Heaven and the former earth had passed away, and the sea was no more. I also saw the holy city, a new Jerusalem, coming down out of Heaven from God, prepared as a bride adorned for her husband. I heard a loud voice from the throne saying, "Behold, God's dwelling is with the human race. He will dwell with them and they will be His people and God Himself will always be with them (as their God). He will wipe every tear from their eyes, and there shall be no more death or mourning, wailing or pain, for the old order has passed away." (Revelation 21:1-4)

You were made for Heaven. My greatest prayer for you and the deepest desire of my heart is that you will be there and that we will all be together in Heaven. I think about this every day. I want you, and your children, and your children's children, and the descendants that I will never see to all be in Heaven. The goal of everything I have ever taught you or done in your life can be summed up in one word: HEAVEN. *Heaven* is what matters most! At the end of your life, you will not worry about money, possessions, or your career. You cannot take anyone or anything with you. Your thoughts will be focused on eternity. You can't imagine the perfect joy, peace, beauty, love, and unity that await you there. It's beyond your wildest dreams. *No eye has seen, no ear has heard, no mind has conceived what God has prepared for those who love Him. (1 Corinthians 2:9)* Heaven is often described as an incredible wedding feast in which Christ is the Bridegroom, and the Church is His Bride. You have already been given an invitation to this wedding—it is a marriage proposal for all eternity because God loves you so much. None of us deserves this incredible gift, and we cannot ever earn our way into Heaven, but God's grace makes it all possible when we accept His invitation.

Of course, you are free to reject the offer. There are no "shotgun" weddings in Heaven. God's love is so perfect that He will never force anyone to accept the gift of Himself. That is why hell is real as well. His Eminence, Raymond Leo Cardinal Burke once told me, "The existence of hell is actually proof of how much God loves us." At first, this seems a strange statement. We might be tempted to think, "What? How can a loving God damn a soul to hell for all eternity? That is cruel!" Not really. Remember this truth: God's love is perfect, and perfect love must be freely given and freely received—no coercion, no manipulation, no pressure, and no force—or else it isn't love at all. If you don't love God and don't *want* to be one with Him, He grants your wish. He does not send you to hell by some cruel verdict or measure by which you failed, but He loves you so much, He allows you to choose it. Does this choice sadden Him? Yes, because you were made to be with Him. Will He do everything in this life, move Heaven and earth, to invite you again and again and again into a relationship of love? Yes. But in the end, He will not force you. He will allow you to remain separated from Him, and that is what hell really is—final separation from God. If you reject His love and grace by your own free will, your hell simply begins here on earth and continues for all eternity. The choice is up to you. Choose wisely.

Finally, I must tell you to be prepared at any moment to enter into eternity. Your life could change on a dime with one misstep into traffic, one accident on the highway, one sudden medical emergency. You must be ready. Live for Heaven *now*. I never thought that I would be so close to meeting my Maker in August 2008 while recovering from a routine surgery. And yet, I found myself "one step away" in an emergency room when a football-sized pool of blood burst in my abdomen. My veins collapsed, I went into shock, and the doctor told me I was "checking out." As I lay naked under a sheet with the realization that I was about to go out and might never wake up, I only wanted to profess my faith in Jesus, ask for forgiveness, and die with His name on my lips. I focused on the promise of salvation and repeatedly said in a loud voice, "Jesus, I trust in you! Jesus, I trust in you!" I didn't care what the doctors or nurses thought of me. I didn't have time to worry about anything else at all. In that moment, the prospect of eternity became *real*. Heaven is the only thing that mattered. Someday you, too, might unexpectedly find yourself "one step away." Are you ready? Do you think about Heaven often? Do you pray for the grace to desire Heaven?

When you live in light of eternity, the little things of everyday life take on a different perspective. It becomes important to say, "I love you," to never let the sun set on your anger, and to quickly ask for forgiveness whenever you sin. Treasure moments with family and friends, express gratitude, help those in need, and live each day as if it were your last. These are the lessons I learned from your Uncle Tom, who knew he was dying and prepared well. If today is my last day, I want to give God glory and honor with everything I think, and say, and do. To my last breath, I want to thank Him for this incredible gift of life and love Him with all my being. How God chooses to bring me home is totally up to Him. I trust His perfect plan for my life *and* my death. I do have one little wish— to die with the name of Jesus on my lips and, as St. Madeleine

Sophie Barat suggests, "to be like the swan: When it is dying it gathers all its inner forces and sings with more harmony than ever before in its life. That is how saints die. It is the purest act of their life, the one most burning with love, the most perfect."

Death is all around us, revealed in the beauty of November, the lessons of nature, and this season of the Church. It is good to ponder these truths and prioritize our lives based on eternity, for life on earth passes quickly. It is just a tiny breath in comparison to the new life that awaits us. I can honestly tell you that as much as I love this life and live it to the full, I can't wait for Heaven. There are so many people I long to see again, so many saints I want to meet. Most of all, I long to experience perfect unity with God and with all mankind. I can't wait to hear the magnificent chorus, to sing and dance like never before, to love and laugh forever, to feast on joy, and praise God with the universe.

Pray for me when I die that God has mercy on my soul and that I will not cling to this world. Pray that I will mount up on eagle's wings and soar into the arms of my Father in Heaven. If you should be at my side, please say the Chaplet of Divine Mercy and the Glorious Mysteries of the Rosary, which focus on Heaven. And remember, I love you so much, I want—more than anything else in the whole world—for us to be together for all eternity. Heaven is what matters most!

♥ Mom

November 18, 2011
Feast of St. Rose Philippine Duchesne

Chapter 4

Jesus Christ—and why I want you to put Him first

"Do not be afraid of Christ! He takes nothing away, and He gives you everything. When we give ourselves to Him, we receive a hundredfold in return. Yes, open, open wide the doors to Christ—and you will find true life."
(Pope Benedict XVI, Mass of Inauguration, April 24, 2005)

Dear John, Julie, and Kevin,

Today is a special anniversary, and I want to share with you my joy! Exactly ten years ago, I began a spiritual journey that changed my life forever. On January 7, 2002, our entire family attended a parish mission by the Apostles of the Interior Life. It was here that I first heard the invitation to search for holiness in my everyday life. The sisters planted the seeds in my heart to fall deeper in love with our Lord Jesus Christ, to follow Him more closely, to commit to a life of prayer, and to put Jesus first–above all things. For the past ten years, I have experienced firsthand what it means to "open wide the doors to Christ" and to find true life. This has been the greatest adventure of my life! I never imagined that I could experience so much joy in His presence and feel His love surrounding me at all times. It is impossible to recount all that Jesus has done or how my life is different since falling in love with Him. Nevertheless, I want to tell you about Jesus in my own words and reveal to you my heart that belongs to Him.

My own relationship with Jesus is so personal–fostered in the solitude and silence of daily prayer–that I don't often talk about it. For the past ten years, however, I have poured out my heart and soul in the pages of over sixty journals written to Jesus, with Jesus, for Jesus, and about Jesus. To you or to any outsider, my entries might seem strange, but I can't help trying to articulate this fire from within that is the love of Jesus Christ.

> "Lord, I feel your presence. I hear you call my name–so personally, so lovingly, so uniquely your voice inside of me. You gently nudge me to your truth, gently invite me to abandon my sins and silly attachments, to totally surrender everything, and simply rest in your arms. Thanks for whispering in my heart. Thanks for revealing your plan for my life, step by step, and weaving this unbelievable tapestry of people and events– one thread at a time. Thank you for your call and the joy of hearing your voice. Thank you for this relationship of love. I don't deserve it. I fail you every day. But I am so drawn to you, Jesus. I am like a moth to a flame. I can't get enough of your grace, of your mercy, of your love. I want to remain in your embrace and continually live in your peace and joy!" (Journal

entry: March 25, 2008–9:45 a.m. in the waiting room at
the oral surgeon's office)

Page after page, volume after volume, I never tire of
praising Jesus, thanking Jesus, and sharing my heart with Jesus.
Often, I simply write "JOY!" in huge letters across the page
because no other word comes close to what I am feeling.
However, these prayer journals only scratch the surface of my
love for Him. I hope that my entire being and all my actions
reveal–far greater than any words ever could–that Jesus Christ is
the Son of God, the Second Person of the Blessed Trinity, the
Eternal Word made Flesh, the long-awaited Messiah, the King of
kings, the Lord of lords, the Savior of the World, the Prince of
Peace, my Redeemer, my Rock, my Strength, the Lover of my
soul, the Light of my life, the Joy of my heart, my Refuge, my
Friend, my Teacher, my Mentor, the Center of my life, my
Everything, my *All in All*, the Alpha and the Omega, the
Beginning and the End.

Even if I don't say it every day, I hope you know this
one essential truth about the source of my joy and the
foundation of my life: *I live by faith in the Son of God, who has
loved me and given Himself up for me. (Galatians 2:20)* Any good
that I do is only with Him, in Him, and through Him. It's all
Jesus. My hope for Heaven is all because of His Redemption;
my love for you and for your father is an extension of His self-
giving love revealed on the Cross; my enthusiasm for life is His
Holy Spirit living inside of me; my gifts and talents are only a
means to point to Christ. I seek to love Jesus above all things
and serve Him as I live out my vocation as wife and mother.
This is my joy! In the ordinary and extraordinary moments of
life, I want to sing of His salvation, praise His name, and thank
Him—and then continue doing the same in Heaven for all
eternity.

I want to assure you that life with Jesus is never boring! I often experience Jesus as the Good Shepherd, who leads me to green pastures, protects me, and provides for my every need—often in ways that I never dreamed possible. *I am the Good Shepherd. A good shepherd lays down his life for the sheep ... I know mine and mine know me. (John 10:11, 14)* In college, the Good Shepherd led me to the University of Missouri-St. Louis (UMSL), although I did *not* want to go there at all. I wanted to seek out the "pastures" of St. Louis University which seemed more exciting. However, Jesus was already providing for my future, and He led me exactly where I needed to go. First, He led me to Germany, which was far more exciting than simply going to St. Louis University. Then, He led me to your father and to my first teaching job, all by the grace of attending UMSL.

You, too, at times have been led to where you did not want to go. John and Kevin, you have felt the sting of being cut from athletic teams and passed over by coaches; you have also known loneliness when friends moved away or friendships simply changed. Julie, when your dance studio abruptly closed, your special group of friends was scattered and your beloved dancing "home" was gone for good; you were forced to move on. Hopefully, you have come to realize, however, that Jesus carries you in His arms as He leads you to where you were *meant* to be. He gives you new dreams and sweet consolations as well. Trust Jesus and follow where He leads. He knows you better than you know yourself. He knows the desires of your heart, and He knows the plan for your life.

Also, I want to encourage you to seek Jesus in all things and recognize Him in the tiny details of your daily life. He is always near—closer than you might think—living and working inside of you and in the faces of those you meet. Recognize Jesus in the cashier at the grocery store, the stranger standing in line, or the waiter at a restaurant. So many circumstances present themselves as opportunities to love Jesus, if only to hold the door open for an elderly person or to assist a young mother with her children. *"Amen," I say to you, "whatever you did for one of these least brothers of mine, you did for me." (Matthew 25:40)* Every smile takes on a deeper meaning, every frustration born out of love for Jesus has value, and every menial task becomes an offering of love. Invite Jesus into your heart, yes! But also invite Him into your busy schedule, your friendships, and ordinary activities. Becoming aware of His presence at all times and in all people will transform your days into countless moments of grace and unexpected blessings.

In recent years, I have been drawn to Jesus in the elderly, the lonely, and the dying—though it was difficult for me at first. In September 2007, I was scared to death when I visited the Women's Correctional Facility in New England, North Dakota, for the first time. I had no idea what I was going to say to this group of women as I walked through the prison doors. Yet after the allotted hour, we were exchanging hugs and tears, and I did not want to leave. I had found Jesus in their tears of loneliness and yearning for authentic love. Their faces are still etched in my memory.

I was also nervous this past summer at a family reunion when I first met Judy, one of your father's many cousins. Because the family is so big, I had never actually seen her, much less spoken with her in all these years. She came to the reunion, however, because she knew it would be her last due to the progression of Lou Gehrig's disease. Although Judy could no longer walk or talk, it was wonderful to finally meet her. As I placed my hands into the hollowed palms of her deteriorating hands, I felt the wounds of Christ—as real to me as if I were present at Calvary. I had found Jesus in Judy, and I wanted to spend as much time with her as possible. That was the beginning of our weekly visits and the birth of a beautiful friendship. Again and again, I am drawn to His love, revealed in the faces of those who are right next to me in the most unexpected places. You might find yourself drawn to Jesus in the poor, the homeless, the handicapped, or the outcast. He is there, for sure, and in countless other faces as well. Pray for the grace to recognize Him.

Finally, I want to share with you the way in which I experience Jesus most powerfully and most intimately: I am drawn to Jesus in the Holy Eucharist. It is in the Eucharist where Jesus, The Bread of Life, sustains me with His love, nourishes my soul with His divine life, and gives me the gift of His very self. What a joy, what an honor, what a privilege it is to physically *taste and see the goodness of the Lord!* (*Psalm 34:8*) I want you to know that I love receiving Jesus in the Eucharist at daily Mass. I don't *have* to go to Mass; I *want* to go because Jesus, by the power of the Holy Spirit, comes down from Heaven, becomes physically present under the appearance of bread and wine, and promises eternal life for those who receive Him. *Unless you eat the flesh of the Son of Man and drink His blood, you do not have life within you. Whoever eats my flesh and drinks my blood has eternal life, and I will raise him on the last day.* (*John 6:53-54*) I witness a miracle every morning—more amazing than the sunrise—and am filled with awe and wonder as I ponder this incredible gift. Jesus invites us to participate in the eternal Wedding Feast of the Lamb and be united with Him in His Body and Blood. It is my joy to believe and say, "Yes!"

As you mature into adulthood, I pray that Jesus will become the center of your life and the joy of your heart. I pray that you will seek Him, fall in love with Him, and put Him first above all things—above your job, money, other relationships, activities, sports, and leisure. Your relationship with Jesus, like any relationship of love, will require sacrifice, time together, and perseverance to maintain. *But the one who perseveres to the end will be saved. (Matthew 24:13)* No doubt, perseverance is *the* challenge, but look no further than your father as an example of one who puts Jesus first—even when it is not easy:

John, when you were fifteen years old and had been playing baseball for nine straight years, we were tired of driving, tired of baseball, and tired of out-of-town tournaments. I remember the thrill when another family once offered to take you to a weekend tournament 150 miles away. Your dad was ecstatic and looked forward to a rare weekend at home completely free! Then he realized that it might not be possible for you to go to Mass. Games were scheduled straight through Saturday night and began again at 9:00 on Sunday morning. No other family on the team would take you to Mass at the crack of dawn on Sunday morning, and you could quite possibly arrive home late Sunday night if you advanced in the tournament—too late for a Sunday evening Mass back home. Your father called the family and declined their generous offer. He changed his plans, packed his Sunday clothes, drove for hours, and sat through all your games in the sweltering heat. He paid over $200 for meals and two nights in a hotel. On Sunday morning, he found the local Catholic Church and took you to 7:00 Mass before any games started that day. He sacrificed his entire weekend so that you would not miss Mass. That is why I love and respect your father so much. He puts Jesus first—above sports, above his own schedule, above money, and convenience. I hope you follow in his footsteps.

All I can tell you is, "It's worth it!" When you give your life to Him, you will receive a hundredfold. St. Rose Philippine Duchesne said it better: "If you have Jesus, you have everything." Jesus Himself said it the best: *I am the Way and the Truth and the Life. No one comes to the Father except through me. (John 14:6)* Life with Jesus is filled with hope, peace, strength, joy, and love. He is with you in your trials, He is comfort in your sorrows, and

He knows exactly what you are going through. If you ever find your love growing cold or indifferent, stare at a crucifix and ponder the nails that pierced Him. Pray the Stations of the Cross and picture Jesus carrying the heavy beams. Watch the movie *The Passion of the Christ,* read the Passion narrative from the Gospels, and think of Jesus hanging for three hours on the Cross for you. How can you possibly respond to such love? Love Him in return with all your heart, soul, mind, and strength. Trust Him with your very life. Put Him first.

I wish you all the love—and the joy—that is found in Jesus!

Mom

January, 7, 2012
Feast of St. Raymond of Peñafort

Chapter 5

The Catholic Church—and why I want you to love it

"You possess the Holy Spirit to the extent that you love the Church."
(St. Augustine)

Dear John, Julie, and Kevin,

One of the most beautiful gifts of my life was being born and raised in a Catholic family with aunts, uncles, cousins, and grandparents who were all Catholic as well. Through no choice of my own, I have been blessed to celebrate life's most important moments focused on Jesus, in the context of the Church, surrounded by a huge Catholic family. Baptisms, First Communions, Confirmations, weddings, and funerals have all been great occasions of unity and faith throughout my life. I can't imagine life without the Church, the Sacraments, or the rhythm of the liturgical seasons. I can't fathom any major holiday—Thanksgiving, Christmas, 4th of July, or Easter—without first celebrating Mass and then gathering with extended family. This is my heritage, my identity. It's in my blood, handed down from a long line of Catholic ancestors.

My First Communion

Because your father had a similar upbringing and strong Catholic identity as well, there was never any doubt that we would raise you in the Catholic Church and pass this heritage on to you. We never gave it a second thought. And so began your life of Catholic schools, Catholic athletic programs, Catholic scouting, Catholic youth groups, Catholic retreats, and Catholic friends. Your entire upbringing, family life, social life, and formation have been centered in the Catholic Church and parish activities.

Off to St. Ferdinand School

Julie's Confirmation

John's First Communion   Kevin's Confirmation

But that isn't enough. It's certainly not a free ticket into Heaven, nor a guarantee that you will stay in the Church, live a moral life, or strive for holiness.

Your Catholic identity and education will only take you so far. At some point you will ask yourself, "Do I really believe *everything* that the Church teaches? Do I want to remain Catholic *forever*? Do I want to practice this Catholic faith when it doesn't fit with my lifestyle or when the demands are too high? What if I like going to a different church, where I prefer the preaching or contemporary music? Does it *really* matter if I am Catholic? Aren't all denominations equal?" If you haven't already done so, you will probably ask similar questions some Sunday morning when you are away at college. You might confront these questions again when you get your first job, move out on your own, meet new friends, stay out late, work all night, or go on vacation. No one will be looking over your shoulder. You will be free to decide for yourself whether to go to Mass or not.

Ultimately, however, your decision to live your life as a Catholic Christian will come down to one more crucial question: Do you love Jesus Christ *and* His Church? Many people simply ask the first part, "Do you love Jesus?" Isn't that enough? And if you only knew about the first part—Jesus only—then the answer is "yes." But once you know the whole story about Jesus, the nature of Jesus, and the Church He established, then the answer is "no." You can't separate the two. To love Jesus, is to love His Church, and to love His Church—the Body of Christ, His Bride—is to love Jesus. Jesus established one Church—the Catholic Church. If you are to remain Catholic, ultimately, you will have to confront both parts of the question: Do you *love* Jesus Christ *and* His Church?

I danced around this question until I was thirty-six years old. Despite my strong Catholic upbringing and outward obedience, I had taken my faith and Catholic identity for granted. No one would have ever guessed. I did everything a good Catholic should do: I went to Mass every Sunday and on Holy Days of obligation; I gave my time, talent, and treasure to the Church; I prayed and observed days of fasting and abstinence from meat; I attended Holy Thursday and Good Friday services; I sent you to the parish school; I volunteered for practically every committee possible and led the congregation in song every week as cantor. There was just one tiny thing. Out of everything in the Catholic Church, there was only one law I did not follow, just one, small, side issue that I thought was no big deal—contraception. In secret, I was dissenting from the Catholic Church, but justified my use with many arguments: "I was following my own conscience. This was a man-made law that I could ignore. Contraception was a private decision between me, my husband, and God. The Church really had no business in this matter, and it had *nothing* to do with my faith or love of God." Or so I thought.

My struggles with the Church's teaching on contraception would eventually lead to a much larger issue and cause me to wrestle with my entire Catholic identity. But soon, I was confronted with the very idea of what it meant to be a Catholic Christian, and why it mattered. One homily by Fr. Gary Gebelein triggered the crucial question when he quoted St. Augustine and said, "You possess the Holy Spirit to the extent that you love the Church." And I sat there, somewhat taken aback, because I knew I did not love *the* Church. I could, however, think of a million things that I loved *about* our local church: the fun of parish picnic, our wonderful pastor, the excellent parish school, great parishioners, a good choir, active organizations, my involvement as cantor and Bible school teacher, etc. I loved many things *about* our church, but I did not love *the* Church. I didn't like all of her teachings—much less love them. Specifically, I did not like the moral teachings, which seemed burdensome and unfair. Also, I felt Rome was out of touch with my real world. All I wanted was to go to church on Sunday, send my children to the Catholic school, consider ourselves to be a good Catholic family, and not worry about the rest. Was it truly necessary to *love the Church?* Couldn't I just love God and Jesus? Wasn't that enough?

The question of Jesus and His Church became the turning point of my spiritual journey, and my life has never been the same, both in private and in public. I have simply fallen in love with Jesus Christ *and* His Church and want to serve Jesus in the Church for the rest of my life. Do I desire this for you? Yes, I do. I pray that you will discover for yourself the beauty and richness of the Catholic Church. I also hope that you will fall in love with the Church and understand why it matters that you are a Catholic Christian. I hope your Catholic faith is not just some book knowledge or some familial identity that you wear on holidays and special occasions, but rather a burning love that transforms how you think, what you do, and how you will live. And so, to the heart of the matter: *Why Catholicism?* What is there to love in this seemingly male-dominated, antiquated, hierarchical, legalistic, ritualistic, historically corrupt Church? How can I possibly declare that I love the Roman Catholic Church, and why should you? Let me count the ways!

First, the Catholic Church is *one.* Jesus Himself established one Church when he gave Peter the keys to the Kingdom of Heaven and said: *You are Peter, and upon this rock I will build my Church. (Matthew 16:18)* Notice, "Upon this rock I will build *my* Church." He did not say, "I will build *your* Church," nor did he say, "I will build *many* Churches." No. Jesus is very clear. He established one Church, and declared it to be His. In Scripture, this relationship between Jesus and His Church is often described as the relationship between the Bridegroom and His Bride. What is the relationship between a bridegroom and his bride? It is a one flesh union, impossible to divide. *Christ loved the Church and gave Himself up for her, that He might sanctify her. (Ephesians 5:25-26)* Therefore, when we love the Church, we are imitating Jesus Himself, and recognizing the truth that He is one with His Bride. Unity is the essence of His Church, and this only makes sense when we think of the Son of God in union with the Trinity, who desires union and communion with us. Jesus prayed at the Last Supper *that they may be one. (John 17:21)* He assured us that *there will be one flock, one shepherd. (John 10:16)* In St. Paul's letters to the early Christians, he repeatedly urged *that there be no divisions among you, (1 Corinthians 1:10)* to *avoid those who create dissensions, (Romans 16:10)* and to *complete my joy by being of same mind, with the same love, united in heart, thinking one thing. (Philippians 2:2)*

Where throughout 2000 years of Christianity can you find such unity? Where can you find visible bonds of unity specifically in doctrine, worship, and governance? In the Catholic Church. Think about ordinary life for a minute: Every school has its principal; every school district has its superintendent; every company has its CEO; every city has its mayor; every state has its governor; and every nation has its president, chancellor or king. Why? Without a visible leader, chaos ensues, everyone does his or her own thing, and unity is shattered into a million pieces. Jesus, the Good Shepherd, knew this. He would not leave His sheep without a shepherd. Therefore, Jesus gave Peter primacy over all the Apostles to teach, to lead, and to unify the early Church when inevitable arguments arose. Two thousand years later, we are still united in the Catholic Church under Peter's successor. I love it!

Second, the Catholic Church is *holy*, which means it is a divine institution, guided by the Holy Spirit as the Guardian of all truth, and nothing shall prevail against it. This is, by far, the Church's most outrageous claim of all. If it is true, then as the Bride of Christ in perfect union with her Bridegroom, I can believe her every word, rely on her teachings, and trust her forever. If it is not true, then the Catholic Church is the most despicable of liars, and I want no part of it. How can I know? How can I be so sure? I trust in Jesus.

In John's Gospel, Jesus promised that the Father will *give you another Advocate to be with you always, the Spirit of truth. (John 14:16-17) The Advocate, the Holy Spirit that the Father will send in my name–He will teach you everything and remind you of all that I told you. (John 14:26) He will guide you to all truth. (John 16:13)* When He founded His Church and handed the keys to Peter, Jesus also promised that *the gates of the netherworld shall not prevail against it. (Matthew 16:18)* So then, what was the source of truth for the Apostles and early Church Fathers after Jesus ascended into Heaven? It was not the Bible–there was no Bible yet. It was the Church, established on the rock of Peter, which St. Paul called *the pillar and foundation of truth. (1 Timothy 3:15)* St. Irenaeus, writing in approximately the year 200 confirmed this belief: "For where the Church is, there also is God's Spirit; where God's Spirit is, there is the Church and every grace." (*Against Heresies* 3, 24, 1)

Were it not for the guidance of the Holy Spirit and the promises of Jesus, the Church would have never lasted. Nero and numerous other Roman emperors tried to destroy it. They murdered almost every Pope for the first three centuries. Napoleon tried to destroy the Church; Stalin tried as well. They all failed. History has proven that nothing shall prevail against it. No doubt, our own sins throughout history have greatly wounded the Church, but she still stands—in spite of scandal, in spite of abuse, in spite of some terrible Popes, and the sinfulness of every member. At times, the *Parable of the Weeds growing among the Wheat (Matthew 13)* rings painfully true for the Church. Nevertheless, the Catholic Church cannot be divided or destroyed. It cannot be guided by democracy or popularity, but only by the Holy Spirit to preserve truth. Jesus promised this, the Apostles and the early Church Fathers believed it, and so do I.

I came to believe that the Holy Spirit was in fact guiding the Catholic Church when I discovered the beautiful truth about sex and the lies regarding contraception. One particular event from history proved quite interesting: Before 1930, every Christian denomination believed and taught what the Catholic Church taught, namely that contraception was intrinsically evil. The Anglican Church first broke from this teaching in 1930 at the Lambeth Conference. Soon after, so did every other mainline Protestant denomination. By the 1960's, the world waited for the Catholic Church to get with the times, and everyone *thought* Pope Paul VI would simply change the Church's teaching on contraception.

Instead, he shocked the world—at tremendous personal cost—and reaffirmed the truth about love and life when he published the encyclical *Humanae Vitae* in July 1968. It went over like a bomb. Pope Paul VI was ridiculed by the world press and blasted by many Catholic theologians, bishops, and priests. Dissent from within the Church spread among millions of ordinary Catholics. However, the Catholic Church would not cave under pressure when it came to truth and morals. It was guarded from error by the Holy Spirit. Pope John Paul II later affirmed the prophetic truth found in *Humanae Vitae* with his own *Theology of the Body,* and some thirty-five years after *Humanae Vitae* was first published, I found myself surprised by truth and gratefully saying, "The Church was right. Thank God for the Catholic Church—the only institution to courageously uphold and proclaim the truth about sex and marriage for 2000 years."

And so, if the Catholic Church was right about contraception, I could then trust her when faced with competing opinions over countless hot-button issues, such as embryonic stem cell research, same-sex "marriage," abortion, sterilization, euthanasia, and capital punishment. For with every moral dilemma of our day, battles rage in the media, in government, and within families. I find myself asking, "Lord, to whom shall I go? Where can I find truth? What is *your* truth in these complex, difficult questions?" I can't trust the medical profession to have all the answers because they have lost their moral compass. I certainly don't trust any political party for absolute truth, nor do I trust my friends—all of whom are good people, but have varying opinions. I can't look in the Bible to find a clear, definitive answer for embryonic stem cell research or in vitro fertilization. It isn't there. And so, I turn to the Catholic Church, *the pillar and foundation of truth, (1 Timothy 3:15)* to provide clear moral guidance in our troubled and confused world. I love that I can trust her teachings and can depend on her moral courage. When it comes to faith and morals, truth cannot change, for the Church is holy and guided by the Holy Spirit. The powers of hell shall not prevail against it—and that, too, is why I love it!

Third, the Church that Jesus established is *catholic*, which simply means "universal." This is the easiest claim to accept because it is the most visible. With over one billion Catholics around the globe, the Church is definitely worldwide. Her mission is universal in drawing all people to Jesus Christ. *Go therefore and make disciples of all nations, baptizing them in the name of the Father and of the Son and of the Holy Spirit, teaching them to observe all that I have commanded you. And behold, I am with you always, until the end of the age. (Matthew 28:19-20)* The Church successfully embodies the various cultures, races, traditions, and languages in each particular part of the world, proving that diversity and variety of expression are possible, while maintaining unity. *For as in one body we have many parts, and all the parts do not have the same function, so we, though many, are one body in Christ. (Romans 12:4-5)*

I came to appreciate the universality of the Catholic Church when I lived away from home for the first time as an au pair in Munich, Germany. On Sunday mornings, I rode my bicycle to the small neighborhood parish and sat in the dimly lit sanctuary with a dozen or so senior citizens who also came. But the moment I set foot in that church, I was "home" because Jesus was there, present in the tabernacle. I could look around and see the familiar altar, the Stations of the Cross, candles, holy water font, statues, and sanctuary light. Although I was half a world away, I heard the same Old and New Testament readings, the same Responsorial Psalm, and the same Gospel proclaimed from Sacred Scripture that my parents would hear at Mass on the same day back home. And though I didn't speak the language at first, I understood exactly where we were in the Mass Sunday after Sunday. That is an amazing reality. The Mass is the Mass. The prayers are the same.

It is an unbelievable, indescribable feeling to realize that you are receiving the same Eucharist as well. Jesus is made present on every altar in the Holy Sacrifice of the Mass in every Catholic Church the world over. Calvary is re-presented, and I am standing at the foot of the Cross no matter if I am sitting in a grand cathedral in Rome, a tiny church in Africa, or St. Ferdinand Parish in Florissant, Missouri. This is why I first decided to practice the faith from my childhood as an adult. I chose Catholicism and made it my own because I was "home" anywhere in the world within the Catholic Church.

Fourth, the Catholic Church is *apostolic*, which means it was and remains built on the foundation of the Apostles. Jesus, who had been given *all power in Heaven and on earth, (Matthew 28:18)* delegated to His Apostles the authority to preach, teach, heal, legislate, discipline, forgive sins, and speak in His name. From the early Church, the role of priest, bishop, and deacon were all identified and united under Peter as the first of the Apostles. Also noteworthy from the early Church was the replacement of Judas with Mathias. Why replace Judas? Why not just go with eleven good Apostles? Because the office of shepherding the Church was—like Peter's office—permanent. Despite the sinfulness of Judas, the office would endure. Today, it is exercised without interruption by the sacred order of bishops. (*Catechism of the Catholic Church*, 862)

Why does this matter? It matters because the office of Pope and office of bishop have for over 2000 years preserved the faith handed on by Jesus to His Apostles. The celebration of the Eucharist at Mass was not simply invented. No, the Mass was instituted by Jesus at the Last Supper, remembered by His Apostles, celebrated as the focus of Sunday worship in the early

Church, and preserved by the Catholic Church to the present. All of the original Sacraments have been preserved and handed down. Likewise, the Bible didn't drop out of Heaven. No, it was the Catholic Church that determined the Sacred Canon of Scripture, translated it, and preserved it. Because of the authority of the Church, the Catholic Bible remains unchanged in its fullness—with nothing omitted to the present day.

Go to the most sacred places in all of Christianity— where Jesus was born in Bethlehem, where Jesus delivered His *Sermon on the Mount*, where Jesus was crucified on Calvary, where He was buried in the tomb, where Peter was crucified in Rome, where Paul was beheaded—and see for yourself. At all of these holy sites you will find the Catholic Church. Why? Because from the very beginning, the Catholic Church remembers, commemorates, and preserves. Your Catholic roots are visible, tangible, documented by early Church writings, and preserved for 2000 years.

Also, I believe in the authority of the Catholic Church because of the words of Jesus to His Apostles. *Whoever listens to you listens to me. Whoever rejects you rejects me. And whoever rejects me rejects the One who sent me. (Luke 10:16)* This Scripture verse crushed my personal "wall of dissent" and led me to believe everything the Church teaches—as a matter of faith, obedience, and love for Jesus. Once I realized that the Apostles had been given authority by Jesus Himself and that this same mission and authority continued with the unbroken line of succession, I saw clearly: The Catholic Church is the living, active voice of Jesus Christ in the world today. When I listen to the Church, I am listening to the voice of Jesus. If I reject the teachings of the Church, I am rejecting Jesus, and if I ignore the teachings of the Church, I am ignoring Jesus. Even if I don't fully understand, even if I find certain teachings difficult or challenging, I now trust the Church completely to teach, discipline, and legislate in matters of faith and morals. I love the teaching authority of the Church. What a great way to clearly hear the voice of Jesus in the world today!

One, holy, catholic, and apostolic—these are just four basic reasons why I love the Church. But there are more. Beauty and reverence top my list as well. Some of the world's greatest works of art are preserved in Catholic Churches, where breathtaking mosaics, sculptures, stained glass windows, tapestries, and frescos lift countless hearts and souls to God. You have witnessed this timeless beauty in the cathedrals of Rome, Florence, Venice, Siena, Assisi, Paris, Munich, etc. Think of Michelangelo's *Pietà* or the ceiling of the Sistine Chapel, where Heaven meets earth. Inspired by faith, these works of art are preserved for all mankind—the rich and poor, the old and young, the educated and uneducated—to teach the story of salvation.

Pilgrimage to St. Peter's Basilica, Vatican City 2010

In the Catholic Church, our entire being and all our senses are filled with the glory of God through beautiful architecture, art, candles, incense, bells, music, holy water, sacred oils, and the finest of fabrics. We can taste, see, smell, hear, and touch the spiritual and the divine. It is sensual and so beautiful! Some will mock golden chalices, marble statues, and fine vestments as outward show. I, too, once questioned it. Now, I find myself saying, "Bring it on!" I am a physical being, and I want to experience God in and through my senses. Beautiful art, one of the highest forms of human expression, helps us to comprehend the incomprehensible glory of Heaven. It lifts our hearts and minds to God and inspires our worship. Just as God gave specific instructions regarding the adornment of the Ark of the Covenant in the Old Testament, how much more adornment and honor should be given to the very place where Jesus resides. (See *Exodus 25, 26*) The poet John Keats once wrote, "Beauty is truth, truth (is) beauty." When it comes to art found in the Catholic Church, I couldn't agree more.

Obviously, I can still worship Jesus Christ in a simple church, and it's not always about the bricks, mortar, and stained glass windows. But because of the Real Presence of Jesus, Catholics recognize that a church is not just some ordinary gathering space, but rather holy ground. Therefore, I am grateful that even in a modest church my mind is lifted to Heaven with physical reminders of the sacred. I am also grateful that the Catholic Church built some of the most beautiful cathedrals in the world that have stood for centuries as beacons of beauty, reverence, and awe of God. This is one of the reasons why I have taken you on pilgrimages—so that you, too, will appreciate this beauty. You gotta love it!

Finally, I am Catholic because in the Catholic Church I have found the fullness of truth. No doubt, there are elements of truth in all Christian denominations and in all religions of the world. But I want the richness, the fullness, and sacredness of the Church that Jesus established. I want all seven Sacraments, but most especially the Real Presence of Jesus in the Eucharist to be the source and summit of my life. Also, I don't want to be forced to choose between binary options. For example, is Jesus true God or true man? Is the Church human or divine? Is Mary virgin or mother? Do we believe in faith or works? Word or Sacrament? Faith or reason? Sacred Scripture or Sacred Tradition? The answer to all of these questions is *yes* to both parts. For Catholics, the response is *both/and*, not *either/or*. We don't have to choose or settle for half. The fullness of Jesus and the fullness of Christianity are found in both.

The story of *The Road to Emmaus* gives us the perfect example of this fullness that is Catholicism. (See *Luke 24:13-35)* Two men were walking down the road, discussing all that had happened to Jesus. Yet, when our Resurrected Lord appeared and walked along with them, they didn't recognize Him. So what did Jesus do? Jesus interpreted all the Scriptures referring to Him, beginning with Moses and all the prophets. This was awesome! These men were so moved, their hearts were burning! They wanted to continue walking with Him and urged Him to stay, but they were still *clueless* that Jesus was in their midst. Talking about Scripture was great, but it wasn't enough for them to understand *fully*. Only when Jesus took bread, said the blessing, broke it, and gave it to them were their eyes opened, and they finally recognized Him. Only in the breaking of the bread, the Sacrament of the Eucharist! This is exactly what takes place at every Catholic Mass. First, the Word is proclaimed and interpreted. Then, Jesus reveals Himself in the Sacrament. The fullness of Jesus is found in *both*.

Regarding faith and works, we are reminded in the Bible the importance of faith *working through love (Galatians 5:6)* and that *faith without works is dead. (James 2:26)* Again, we see that both faith *and* works are a response to God's grace. Look to Sacred Scripture itself to see if we should hold fast to Scripture alone or Scripture plus Sacred Tradition: *I praise you because you remember me in everything and hold fast to the traditions, just as I handed them on to you. (1 Corinthians 11:2) Stand firm and hold fast to the traditions that you were taught, either by an oral statement or by a letter of ours. (2 Thessalonians 2:15)* The answer, once again, is *both*.

One of my favorite analogies regarding the fullness of Christianity came from listening to a program on Catholic radio. I don't remember the name of the speaker, but he compared our life's journey toward Heaven to a trip across the ocean. The Catholic Church is the cruise ship that has everything on board we could possibly need to carry us on the journey across the stormy waters of life and into the safe harbor of Heaven: Sacred Scripture and Sacred Tradition, faith and reason, Word and Sacrament, etc. Other denominations take one or two aspects from the Catholic Church and hold fast to them alone, while disregarding all the rest—similar to holding onto a raft taken from the cruise ship. They can make it across the ocean to the other shore, but why would I want to hold on to a raft when I could be sailing on the cruise ship? I want all of Jesus—in His Sacraments, in His Word, in the holy Tradition of the Apostles, in the authority of His teachings, in His Real Presence at Mass, exemplified in the lives of the saints, through art, and 2000 years of unity. I want it all, and in the Catholic Church, it's all there.

Warning: It won't be easy or popular for you to remain a Catholic Christian in today's world. You will be misunderstood, insulted, mocked, and perhaps even hated—especially if you uphold the moral teachings of the Church. Be strong and take courage. You are in good company. *If the world hates you, realize that it hated me first. (John 15:18) Rejoice and be glad, for your reward will be great in Heaven. (Matthew 5:12)* At the same time, you must *always be ready to give an explanation to anyone who asks you for a reason for your hope. (1 Peter 3:15)* There is a reason for everything we believe and do in the Catholic Church. Know your faith well and be ready to defend it.

Now you know why I have raised you to be Catholic. The Catholic Church is the one true Church that Jesus Christ established to be His Bride—divine in nature, guided by the Holy Spirit, eternal, universal, apostolic, holy, and the pillar and foundation of truth. Within the Church is the fullness of Christianity in all her beauty as well. Indeed, the Bride is adorned for her Bridegroom! That's why I love the Church. That's why I am Catholic and want our family to remain Catholic. That's why I hope you, too, will love the faith that has been handed down to you. Live it to the full, defend it, and pass it on. Remember who you are—you are a beloved child of God, born into a great Catholic family, redeemed by Jesus Christ. Your ancestors persevered in faith and handed down this incredible legacy for you. It's in your blood. Wow! What a gift! Treasure it always.

Mom

December 16, 2011
Feast of St. Adelaide

Chapter 6

Confession—and why I want you to go often

"Happy the sinner whose fault is removed, whose sin is forgiven."
(Psalm 32:1)

Dear John, Julie, and Kevin,

Many sports fans, like your father, love to reminisce and recall the most important game of their life. They can remember vivid details of that particular day—the opposing team, the location, the players, the unforgettable comeback, or the dramatic finish. Some folks can easily recall their first day on the job, their most important performance, or other life-changing moments with unbelievable precision. The common question, "Where were you on 9/11?" reflects this phenomenon. Such events have a huge physical, emotional, intellectual, and psychological impact on our lives. Therefore, we remember minute details of the entire day. Life is changed from then on.

Looking back over my life, I can recall many wonderful, life-changing moments with vivid detail: On Friday, November 13, 1987, your father took me to dinner at *The Old Spaghetti Factory* and then proposed as we rode together in a white horse-drawn carriage through the cobblestone streets of downtown St. Louis. On July 22, 1988, we were married at St. Norbert Catholic Church. We chose Scripture readings from *Jeremiah 32, Psalm 118, 1 John 4, and Matthew 5* (about salt and light) to be read during the Mass. Our reception was held in the parish gymnasium, packed with 375 guests, costing $3.75 per plate. After twenty-three years, I can still remember the name of the photographer, the DJ, the florist, and the caterer. Typical of many mothers, your birthdates and the exact time of your birth will be forever etched in my memory as well. These were life-changing moments for sure.

However, many more dates immediately stand out as unforgettable as well, including January 25, 2002, July 17, 2007, and January 6, 2009. Nothing earth-shattering happened in the world on any of these dates; I did not experience any tragic accident, joyful surprise, or unexpected news. And yet, I can tell you everything that happened, how I felt, what I did, and where I went. What do these days have in common? Why do I consider them so memorable and life-changing? Confession. Some of the most important, unforgettable, powerful moments of my life have taken place in the Sacrament of Reconciliation, where I experience time and time again God's grace and mercy, His healing, and love. It's physical. It's concrete. My sins are gone, a burden is lifted, and I am set free to be the person I want to be. When I walk out of that confessional, I am a new creation in Christ. I am forgiven and loved. These are life-changing moments for sure.

"Jesus, thank you for the Sacrament of Reconciliation! Everything I try to do is in vain if I know I need to go to Confession, and yet procrastinate. Nothing is right. But I am a new person again this morning, living in your freedom and Redemption. Thank you for your victory over my sins and your power to destroy them— crush them forever! By your grace, I am re-born and saved from the power of darkness. Joy returns. Light illuminates. Grace overflows. Thank you, Jesus, for this incredible gift!" (Journal entry: January 6, 2012)

As you mature in your faith, I hope you will come to appreciate the genius of this Sacrament and your desperate need for it. Every human being needs Confession, and Jesus Christ knew this. That is why on the evening of His Resurrection, He instituted the Sacrament of Reconciliation when He first appeared to his disciples: *"Peace be with you. As the Father has sent me, so I send you." And when He had said this, He breathed on them and said to them, "Receive the Holy Spirit. Whose sins you forgive are forgiven them, and whose sins you retain are retained." (John 20:21-23)* You may question the need to confess your sins to a priest. Remember, however, it is Jesus Himself who gave His disciples the authority by the power of the Holy Spirit to forgive sins. He set it up this way, knowing exactly what you and I—and all of humanity—needed.

"Sin resides primarily in the soul, but secondarily, it resides in every nerve and cell and fiber of our being— and in every corner of our brain. No human being feels satisfied with uneasiness in his heart, where it rankles and festers. All nature speaks for release, and conscience shouts its claim. A foreign substance gets in the stomach that the stomach cannot assimilate; the stomach revolts and casts forth the cause of trouble. A speck gets into the eye, and through pain and tears the eye demands that the dust be removed. Conscience is no different. Every sin seeks release! Most people today have a load on their minds because they have a load on their consciences; the Divine Psychologist knew how miserable we should be if we could not unload that burden. Hospitals are built because people have sick bodies, and the Church builds confessionals because they also have sick souls. Regular Confession prevents our sins, our worries, our fears, our anxieties from seeping into the unconscious and degenerating into melancholy, psychosis, and neuroses. The boil is lanced before the pus can spread into the unconsciousness. The Divine Master knew what is in humanity, so He instituted this Sacrament, not for His needs, but for ours. It was His way of giving us a happy heart." (Archbishop Fulton Sheen, *Peace of Soul)*

We were never meant to carry around our sins which weigh us down. Through the Sacrament of Reconciliation, God lovingly removes the burden. A childhood story, told by British author John Pridmore, has helped me to understand what this Sacrament is all about: When John was a young boy, his mother told him not to play in her rose garden. One day, while he was playing in the backyard, he kicked a ball straight into the roses. As he retrieved the ball, he was stuck by many thorns, one of which lodged itself under the skin of his thumb. For three days, his thumb hurt. It began to swell, throb, and turn red, but he didn't dare show it to his mother for fear of being caught and punished. Finally, after days of avoiding his mother, she noticed and asked, "John, what is wrong with your thumb?" He nervously held out his hand, wondering if she would yell at him. To his surprise, all she said was, "Here, let me take that out for you." And without saying another word, she lovingly removed the thorn from his throbbing thumb.

That is exactly what God wants to do for you—remove the "thorn in your thumb" so that it won't get swollen and infected. The question is: Will you avoid the remedy? Do you think that you can hide the "thorn" or that it will go away on its own? Or, will you run to the One who can remove it for you? Although you don't remember, your own experiences as toddlers were somewhat similar. All three of you loved to play outside in the sandbox with the older neighborhood kids. When one of the neighbors would tell me that you had a dirty diaper, I would come to get you. You, however, would run in the opposite direction. You didn't want to stop, come inside, or be changed. And yet, you reeked! I had to come after you and even chase you at times—all for a simple diaper change. Through the years, I changed hundreds of your dirty diapers, but what I remember most is that I sang to you, kissed you on the cheek, swept you up in my arms, hugged you, patted your fresh bottom, and then sent you back out to play. While changing diapers, I also taught you prayers and nursery rhymes; I spoke to you and giggled with you. Looking back, I fondly remember how intimate those times were. When I see you now, I don't think of you in terms of how many diapers I changed. I only see how much you have grown and how much I love you.

This simple aspect of parenting has taught me so much about the Sacrament of Reconciliation, for if a mother's love causes her to instantly drop whatever she is doing to change a diaper without a second thought, then how much infinitely more does God love us and want to *change* us? It's also taught me about the nature of sin and the need for frequent Confession—at least once a month. My sins reek in the sight of God! I make a mess of things all the time, just like a child. But God, like any good parent, simply wants to *change* me. He doesn't want me to walk around with my messes. He doesn't want any "thorn" to remain stuck in my thumb. So now, I run to Him. I run to Him in the Sacrament of Reconciliation, where I ask Him to remove those things I despise within myself. When I hear His words of absolution, I am immersed in His ocean of mercy. Every Confession for me is a glorious, intimate encounter with my Father who loves me, puts a ring on my finger, kisses me, hugs me, and then sends me back out into the world so that I can be the person I was meant to be. I can't be the wife and mother I want to be, I can't give the speech I was meant to give, nor enjoy the vacation I was meant to enjoy if there is sin weighing on my conscience. I run to the Sacrament of Mercy as quickly as possible, day or night, at home or on the road. I'll do whatever it takes to find a priest who will hear my Confession because it is worth it—every time. I learned this lesson firsthand during one of the most memorable confessions of my life:

At the break of dawn on Monday, July 16, 2007, Julie and I were scheduled to depart with St. Ferdinand's Girl Scout Troop for Minneapolis, Minnesota, and join 3,000 other scouts for a week-long jamboree on the campus of St. Olaf University. By 6:00 a.m., however, I was already disappointed in the leadership and frustrated by the lack of organization in the St. Louis bus caravan. Check-in took over one hour. Then, we sat on the parking lot and waited while the three directors ate breakfast at the McDonalds next door. After what seemed like an eternity, we were finally allowed to board the buses. I started fuming. My behavior—specifically my mouth—spun out of control. I let my disdain show at every rest stop, where we had to put on our Girl Scout sashes just to use the bathrooms. I complained and cursed when we stopped for lunch at 10:30 in the morning. I ignored the rules forbidding snacks on the bus and defiantly ate peanuts all afternoon just to prove how ridiculous the rules were. I called my friends and told them that I was on the "bus trip from hell" with directors who were "Bus-

Nazis." This went on all day and night as I became more and more vocal, even after we arrived at the hotel. At 10:00 p.m., I was still criticizing every detail and complaining about the directors when one of the moms quietly commented, "We didn't have to organize the trip. We didn't have to do any of the work. All we had to do was show up, so I'm just going to try and enjoy it." Her truthful words, spoken in genuine love, pierced me.

Immediately, I felt awful and realized how obnoxious I had been all day. No one else on the bus had complained. No one else had broken the rules or called anyone a "Bus-Nazi." I was ashamed of my behavior and the poor example I had set as the leader for our girls. After apologizing to the co-leaders and parent chaperones, I went to the exercise room to run on the treadmill. I wanted to re-focus, sweat it all out, and get these negative thoughts out of my mind. I prayed for a new attitude and a new beginning as I ran three miles. But it wasn't enough. All the sweat in the world would not absolve me from my sin.

At 5:00 a.m. the next morning, I lay awake, restless and uneasy. Back on the treadmill I went and said from the depth of my soul, "Lord, show me my sin." In that moment, I saw and felt the weight of my ugliness, filth, pride, disobedience, arrogance, and impatience. I remember exactly what I whispered in my heart: "Lord, I need Confession. You know I need Confession. I have to speak tonight at the University of St. Thomas, but how can I possibly speak of 'living water' when I am filled with so much 'vinegar?' I need Confession, but I have to be a Girl Scout leader today, get on a bus, go to the Mall of America at 10:00 a.m., get picked up by a driver at 6:00 p.m., and give a talk tonight. I don't have a car. I have no idea where a nearby Catholic Church might be, and I don't know any priests in Minneapolis. How are you going to work this out when I am at the mercy of my drivers—and a crazy schedule?"

At 10:00 a.m. sharp, as our troop walked into the Mall of America, I remembered the name of a young priest whom I had briefly met two years earlier. We had been introduced at your cousin's First Holy Communion party in Woodbury, Minnesota. It was a long shot, but I sat on a bench outside of the Mall of America, called your Aunt Diane to ask for his phone number, and nervously called the rectory. To my surprise, Fr. James Adams answered the phone, and although I felt like an absolute fool, I began:

"Hello, Fr. James, this is Patty Schneier from St. Louis, Missouri. I am the sister-in-law of Diane Kemper from St. Ambrose of Woodbury Catholic Church, and you probably don't remember, but I met you two years ago at David's First Communion party. I am in Minneapolis and am speaking tonight at the University of St. Thomas. Diane mentioned that this talk was publicized in your parish bulletin. You wouldn't happen to be going to that talk, would you?"

(Long silence ...) "Well, no." More silence continued, as I cringed with embarrassment. He finally said, "I have a Mass for vocations tonight and a banquet immediately following." At this point, I felt ridiculous for having asked the question. In my awkwardness, I only talked faster.

"Oh, I'm sorry to have bothered you. I just thought that if by chance you were going to the talk tonight, I might be able to receive the Sacrament of Reconciliation beforehand."

His tone suddenly changed, and he replied very seriously, "Ohhhhhh ..."

"No, no, no ... Don't get the wrong idea. It's not that big of a deal. I didn't *murder* anybody. I just said some very uncharitable things in the past twenty-four hours, and it is my practice to receive the Sacrament of Reconciliation before I speak. I just went to Confession on Saturday. I'll be fine. I'll say a Rosary, the Chaplet of Divine Mercy, and some extra prayers before I give the talk. It's okay. I'm sorry to have bothered you. If your plans change, here's my cell phone number, but don't worry about it."

Feeling like a complete idiot, I gave him my cell phone number and said goodbye as quickly as possible. I walked into the Mall of America, met up with the group, and put the whole thing out of my mind. I completely switched gears, enjoyed the day at the Mall of America with the Girl Scouts, and then prepared for the talk I was to give that night. My driver was late in picking me up, but as we pulled into the parking lot, my cell phone rang. It was Fr. James Adams. I was totally stunned. He asked, "Where are you, Patty?"

I blurted out, "We are pulling into the parking lot at the University of St. Thomas."

To my utter surprise, he said, "I am driving towards the university right now. I am about *two* minutes away. Which parking lot are you in?"

And without hesitation, I replied, "I have no idea, but I'll stand out on the street corner, so you can find me!"

He pulled up in a Honda, leaned out the window, and said, "Hi, I have ten minutes. Mass just ended, and I must get back to the banquet. Do you mind if we do this right here?"

And without saying a word, he reached over into the glove compartment, pulled out a purple stole, and put it around his neck. I bowed my head, closed my eyes, and collected my thoughts. In my mind, I was no longer sitting in the front seat of a car—I was in the confessional. "Forgive me, Father, for I have sinned. It has been three days since my last Confession ..." (Yes, it had only been three days.) And I wept tears of sorrow, filled with gratitude and joy at the same time, as I unloaded the burden of my sin. I couldn't believe that a priest would go out of his way for a stranger like me and would sacrifice his plans to hear my Confession. What kind of love was this, that he would leave a banquet and start driving toward the university to find me? It was the love of Jesus Christ, and this priest was truly Jesus Christ personified, "*in persona Christi,*" for me. After being absolved, I turned to Fr. Adams and said with all my being, "Thank you for being a priest. I will never forget this Confession as long as I live." I had never felt so personally loved and lavished by God's mercy in all my life. God had brought the Sacrament of Reconciliation to me—in the front seat of a Honda—as a gift, just for the asking. He had heard the silent prayers of my heart—whispered from a hotel treadmill—and had dropped the Sacrament in my lap when I thought it was absolutely *impossible*. I am still blown away at the thought of such mercy and love.

Do you know how much your Heavenly Father wants to forgive you? Do you know to what lengths He will go—just for the asking? Don't ever be too embarrassed to ask for the Sacrament of Reconciliation. No sin is beyond the power of God's forgiveness or worth the weight of its burden. Get rid of it. Be restored to your Father and experience the joy of being saved. This is true peace. This is true freedom. If you sin against any of the Ten Commandments, go to Confession. When you blow it at school or at work, go to Confession. When you snap at the people you love the most, go to Confession. When you are crabby, irritable, and impatient, go to Confession. You will discover that when you experience God's mercy with your own sinfulness over and over again, it becomes easier to forgive others as well. All of your relationships will benefit— but most especially your relationship with God.

The Sacrament of Reconciliation is a precious treasure to be received often—not just once or twice a year. St. Louis, King of France, wrote these parting words of wisdom from his deathbed to his son: "Find a good confessor, and go to Confession often." My thoughts exactly. May you personally encounter the loving mercy of God and the joy of His saving grace in this "Sacrament of a Happy Heart."

♡ mom

January 31, 2012
Feast of St. John Bosco

Chapter 7

The Bible—and why I want you to read it

"The Word of God is living and effective, sharper than any two edge sword, penetrating even between soul and spirit, joints and marrow, and able to discern reflections and thoughts of the heart."
(Hebrews 4:12)

Dear John, Julie, and Kevin,

One of my most treasured memories from your childhood was going to the library every week, filling two huge tote bags with over thirty new books, and "diving" into them as soon as we arrived home. Hours and hours we spent snuggled on the couch as your father and I read aloud your favorite stories, often with tired voices and intermittent yawns. You easily memorized many books and could recite them with unbelievable accuracy. No doubt, *The Berenstain Bears, Curious George,* and *Danny and the Dinosaur* became special "friends" and part of your formation. Those were wonderful moments of carefree, quality time, and I wouldn't trade one second of it now, for all too soon you outgrew my lap and were reading on your own.

John and Kevin enjoy a good book, 1999

Over the years, you have each read Homer and Shakespeare, Chaucer and Dickens, Steinbeck and Mark Twain. You have also read—along with millions of other young enthusiasts worldwide—every book from the *Harry Potter* series. In 2005, you carried with you a brand new copy of *Harry Potter and the Half-Blood Prince* throughout Europe. Julie, in 2007, you pre-ordered the new release of *Harry Potter and the Deathly Hallows.* You eagerly anticipated picking it up upon arrival for the Girl Scout jamboree at the St. Olaf University Bookstore in Minnesota. The following week when we joined the family in Destin, Florida, each of you couldn't wait for your turn to read *Harry Potter* on the beach. We arranged a two-hour reading limit to ensure that each of you received your fair share of book time and had three different book marks to distinguish your place.

You can still quote lines from the *Harry Potter* books because you have read them countless times. The pages are worn and tattered.

After moving on to many other books, you have become avid readers in your own right, and I am proud of you for being so well-read. However, far greater than any book on *The New York Times Best Seller List* or any classic work of literature is the inspired Word of God, the Bible. Nothing compares to the timeless truth and divine revelation that is contained in Sacred Scripture. The Bible is my favorite book on the planet. I consider it the greatest love story ever told, the guidebook for my life, and God's personal message of inspiration every day.

I first came to appreciate the Bible at age eighteen, when I experienced God revealing His Will for my life through the pages of Scripture. Ironically, I was not reading the Bible at that time, nor did I know any other young person who did. As a matter of fact, the *only* person I knew who occasionally read the Bible was my mother. She owned an old, grey-covered Bible with words such as *"thee"* and *"thou"* on every page. I couldn't understand how anyone would want to read this old-fashioned language, much less make any sense of it. However, in December 1983, my life changed—all because my mother read the Bible. I had just been given the opportunity of a lifetime when asked if I wanted to work as an au pair girl in Munich, Germany. I couldn't wait to see the world, venture out on my own, and get out of St. Louis, so I jumped at the chance and immediately said, "Yes!" To my utter dismay, my mother said, "No!" I had never been away from home, never been on an airplane, and didn't speak the language. No one in our family had ever been abroad—no one. Despite my pleading and arguing, she couldn't get over the fear of her young, naïve daughter living with strangers in a foreign country. We were at an impasse. It was awful.

The next night, she couldn't sleep. She got up, went to the kitchen table, randomly opened her Bible, and stared in amazement at what she saw on the page: *The Travels of St. Paul*. It was *not* what she wanted to see, but there it was, this heading in bold print, staring back at her. My mother believed she was meant to read those words as they applied to the difficult parental decision at hand, and in that moment, she knew she had to let me go. God spoke to her heart through the tiniest detail of the Bible, but it was enough to change her mind. The following morning, she gave her consent, and I was free to accept the invitation to live in Europe. Coincidence? Some might think so, but I do not. To this day, I am grateful that my mother read the Bible that night. I am also thankful for her example as a wife and mother who turned to Scripture in times of stress, trusted in God's message, and accepted it—even when it wasn't easy for her.

In my own life, I have experienced time and time again the power of God to reveal truth, to teach lessons, to encourage, and to inspire throughout the pages of Sacred Scripture. Sometimes, the passage I read is exactly what I need to hear at that particular moment, and often I am blown away by God's clear, unmistakable, personal message. However, unlike my mother, I usually do not open the Bible at random. Along with Catholics throughout the world, I read the daily Mass readings of the Church with selections from the Old Testament, the Psalms and Gospels every day. I love this sense of unity and structure, knowing that I am reading the same Gospel as a mother in Uganda, Bolivia, or France on any given day. I put myself into the readings, ponder the scene, and reflect on its meaning as I journal onto the pages of my spiral notebook. I also read *The Word Among Us* and *In Conversation with God* as daily reflection guides. These books challenge me to grow in holiness and help me understand how the daily Scripture readings relate to my everyday life.

> "Lord, today I just praise you for your Word—your timeless message, your personal communication, THE perfect book! I love your Parables, Psalms, Gospels, Paul's letters, etc. You speak with such beautiful imagery and clarity. Life in you really is a treasure. Life in you is a pearl of great price." (Journal entry: August 2, 2006, after reading *The Parable of the Hidden Treasure* and *The Pearl of Great Price.*)

Why do I read the daily readings every day—month after month, year after year? As Pope John Paul II said, "Faith must be constantly strengthened through frequent meditation on God's Word." I want to immerse myself into the Words of Christ, take them to heart, memorize them, and make them my own. Just like the childhood stories that formed your vocabulary, thoughts, and attitudes, I desire to be formed by the Word of God. When difficulties arise and disappointments come my way, I want the Words of Jesus to be on my mind and on my lips.

And so, it is precisely in times of sorrow and distress when I am most grateful for my best friend Terri, who gave me my first Bible and taught me to memorize Scripture. On August 10, 1992, we both chose *1 Thessalonians 5:16* as the goal of our Christian life and memorized it together as our "life's verse." It has been my favorite verse ever since: *Be joyful always, pray constantly, give thanks in all circumstances; for this is God's Will for you in Christ Jesus.* This sums up the kind of person I want to be—one who is joyful always, prays constantly, and gives thanks in all circumstances. So often I fail miserably to live up to this verse in everyday life. However, when we were in Paris and I lost my credit card, my driver's license, and $500 cash, this verse came to mind and gave me a new sense of perspective in the midst of immediate panic. Last summer, when I was diagnosed with both skin cancer and vocal cord damage within the same week, I clung to this Scripture and recalled what I should do—pray and give thanks. It kept me grounded. Time and time again, I rely on Scripture to get me through, to keep me focused, and to remind me of God's truth.

What about you? What are your favorite verses, favorite Parables, and favorite Psalms? Isn't it interesting that we know each other's favorite foods, movies, and activities, but we don't often share our favorites when it comes to Scripture? I love *Psalm 40*, which summarizes my life story, and my favorite Parable is *The Parable of the Mustard Seed* about the tiny seed that becomes the largest bush of all. (See *Matthew 13:31*) Who are your favorite people from the Bible? Jeremiah, Peter, and Paul immediately come to mind as ones who inspire and encourage me, despite their weaknesses. I still get goose bumps every time I read *Jeremiah 20:9* as I relate to his reluctance and fear of public speaking. Whenever I stick my foot in my mouth, I feel just like Peter, who loves the Lord but says the dumbest things at times. Also, it's no coincidence that my conversion occurred on January 25, 2002, on the Feast of the Conversion of St. Paul. Since that day, St. Paul, who was the greatest of sinners, has had a special place in my heart. As for Biblical women, I often feel like Martha with a million things to do, but I desire to be like Mary, who chooses to sit at the feet of Jesus. (See *Luke 10:38-42*)

More than anyone else in Scripture, however, I relate to the Samaritan woman from John's Gospel. After a personal encounter with Christ, she was transformed by His love and the truth He spoke—even the difficult truth regarding the state of her "marriage." It resonated in her heart, and she couldn't resist Jesus' invitation to experience "living water." She also could not contain her joy, and so she left her old water jug at the well and ran into town, telling others about Jesus Christ. (See *John 4:4-26*)

When I first discovered the *Theology of the Body*, this story brought me to tears. I felt just like the woman at the well who was living a lie, but didn't realize it. I, too, was thirsting for more, but I was scared to leave "my old water jug," my old way of life. At the same time, I was so drawn to the beauty of authentic love that I couldn't refuse His invitation to experience marriage as God intended, to find the fulfillment my heart desired, and to never be thirsty again. I wanted to tell others of this truth, but didn't dare. Finally, I could no longer contain my joy and began to share what God had done in my life. Your father gave me a beautiful painting of this scene for Mother's Day that year, and it hangs in our dining room as a remembrance of our journey. The story of *The Woman at the Well* is timeless and life-changing. It's personal for us—and part of our formation.

One thing to remember, however, is that formation is a lifelong process. I could spend my entire life studying, reading, and memorizing Scripture—and only scratch the surface. The more I read, the more I realize how little I know, and that's okay. The joy is in the journey and the discovery of new insights, new lessons, and new inspirations contained within the timeless truths of Scripture. I hope that you become an avid reader of the Bible on your own, that you will find a Bible you love, and that you will write in it, highlight it, and carry it with you. Think of a cell phone. We wouldn't leave for work or go on a trip without our cell phone because it is simply a part of modern life. We need a cell phone to remain "connected" to all that is important, and even though we might silence it for a while or turn it off at certain times, we still check our messages frequently. Imagine if we all thought of the Bible in the same way—that it was a vital part of our daily life, that we wanted to remain "connected" to God, and that we would never leave home without it. Imagine if everyone simply "checked their messages" found in the daily readings of the Church every day. What a wonderful world it would be.

St. Jerome, who first translated the Bible into Latin, said, "Ignorance of Scripture is ignorance of Christ." How true this statement is. Sadly, it describes many Catholics who do not know the Bible. If we are to be a light in this world and draw others to Jesus Christ, then we must be able to walk the walk and talk the talk—and back it up with Scripture. From your earliest years, when you sat on my lap and I read to you stories from *The Beginner's Bible* or sang Bible songs, my hope was that you would always love the Word of God and continue reading it your whole life. Immerse yourself into the Words of Christ and the Heart of Christ. Make His Words your own and part of your vocabulary, for in a very real sense, you become what you read. May you quote Sacred Scripture as easily as you quote your favorite movies, song lyrics, and favorite children's books—and may the pages in your Bible become worn and tattered from countless hours spent in awe of His personal message to you.

Let the Word of Christ dwell in you richly. (Colossians 3:16)

♡ mom

February 6, 2012
Feast of St. Paul Miki and Companions

Chapter 8

Mary—and why I want you to honor her

"Do not fear to take Mary as your Mother on the journey of life! May Mary be a model for you of how to follow Jesus."
(Pope John Paul II)

Dear John, Julie, and Kevin,

When I was a young girl, my "grandmother" Edna frequently told me, "Patty, you are just like your mother!" And I would cringe. Much to my dismay, as I grew older, it became obvious that I was built like my mother as well. My dad, without meaning any harm, would often squeeze my thick, fleshy arms and remind me, "The acorn doesn't fall far from the tree!" Unfortunately, I did *not* take that as a compliment. Typical of many daughters, I did not want to be like my mother.

My mother and I argued frequently during my teenage years, and I wanted to be different—to be more independent, adventuresome, and worldly.

Not until I was older, married, and a mother myself did I come to appreciate what a gift my mother is and what a wonderful, talented person she is. I love her so much and am grateful to have her in my life. My mother has taught me some of life's greatest lessons. She has imparted words of wisdom that have stayed with me to this day, and although I sometimes don't want to hear her advice, it is often the advice I need most. She keeps me grounded, reminds me to

With Mom on my Wedding Day

slow down, and tells me when my priorities are out of balance. When I think of all the times I didn't appreciate her, I am truly embarrassed and ashamed—because she is an awesome mother who only wants what is best for me.

Ironically, my journey with the Blessed Mother is similar. For many years, I did not appreciate Mary as my spiritual Mother. In fact, because I had the Father and the Son, I didn't think I needed a spiritual Mother at all. I did not honor her, say any Marian prayers, nor practice any Marian devotion. I did not own a statue of the Blessed Mother nor have any pictures of her in our home. Mary was for old-fashioned Catholics, for grandmothers who ritualistically clung to their Rosary beads and repeated monotonous, rote prayers. I desperately tried to ignore Mary, to distance myself from her, and label myself as an ecumenical, modern "Bible-Catholic." How foolish I was to disregard the Mother of God, the Queen of Heaven, the Ark of the New Covenant and *my* eternal Mother!

My journey of falling in love with Jesus and the Catholic Church, however, naturally led me to Mary, and though I didn't want to admit it, I gradually came to understand that God had adopted me into His family, and His family included the Blessed Mother:

> "Lord, why are you hitting me over the head with the Rosary? I don't even like the Rosary. I'm not a 'Mary' person. I don't feel like I have to go *through* Mary to get to you! I've lived 36 ½ years, with maybe saying one Rosary that I can remember—when I was twelve years old, and Mike was rushed to the hospital in the middle of the night with the croup. Peggy and I said a Rosary, pacing the living room floor. That's it—once. Now, in just three months, I'm being bombarded with reflections on Mary ... I don't want to be an old-fashioned Catholic. I was born in '65. I'm a Vatican II baby. There was no Marian devotion. I like being an ecumenical Catholic, a 'Bible Catholic,' so that I can walk the walk and talk the talk with Protestants, too. I really don't want to be more Catholic, especially in such an outward, visible sign as holding Rosary beads in public. I'd feel like a fool ...
>
> So, *why*, Lord? Why is my being a *Catholic* Christian important? What about all these rituals, devotions, and outward signs of Catholicism? Are they what remove us from the early Church, or are they sacred, holy traditions which should be preserved? I DON'T KNOW! Is Mary really up there in Heaven next to Jesus 'crowned in glory?' Is she really my spiritual Mother? Do I need a spiritual Mother when I have the Father and the Son? (Is a family complete without a mother?) It can be good without a mother, but it is so much *better* with a mother! Is that what you want me to do,

Lord–just open my eyes to Mary and at least acknowledge her?" (Journal entry: August 8, 2002, Feast of St. Dominic, who was known for his love of the Rosary)

For years I struggled to acknowledge Mary, and I am still growing in this area of faith as I continue to read about the Blessed Mother and learn more about her. Often I have prayed, "Lord, I believe. Help my unbelief when it comes to Mary." You, too, might question why we should honor Mary, why we ask for her intercession, why we pray the Rosary, and why we believe her to be the Immaculate Mother of our Lord and the Queen of Heaven and Earth. These are counter-cultural beliefs to be sure. Because devotion to Mary sets us apart from other Christians and often causes misunderstandings with family and friends, I was hesitant to confront these topics. I behaved like a reluctant teenager who avoids inviting friends over to his house for fear that his mother might embarrass him. This sounds so silly, but it was true. I was a cradle Catholic who avoided all outward signs of Mary for fear of embarrassment, fear of being labeled an "old-fashioned Catholic," and fear of the appearance of false worship. It took a long time, but I can finally articulate with joyful confidence that I honor the Blessed Mother out of love for Jesus and that everything the Catholic Church teaches about Mary makes perfect sense.

There were many seeds of grace that God planted along the way, but two key events in my life broke through my stubbornness and removed the scales from my eyes. The first was on the Eve of Pentecost 2003. I was in St. Ferdinand's Eucharist adoration chapel, reading *Acts 1:13-14* from the daily readings of the Church: The disciples *went to the upper room where they were staying ... and devoted themselves with one accord to prayer, together with some women, and Mary the mother of Jesus, and his brothers.* I began to ponder this scene. The disciples went to the upper room with Mary. Why would they want to be *with* Mary? Perhaps because Jesus had already ascended into Heaven, and the disciples were alone and afraid. In the midst of this fear, they knew that to be at prayer *with* Mary was to be as close to Jesus as humanly possible. And then it hit me. If I wanted to be a disciple of Jesus, then I should do exactly what they did—be at constant prayer *with* Mary. I remember saying in the silence of my heart, "Okay, Mary, pray *with* me. Be with me here in this upper room." I stood up, grabbed a plastic Rosary from the back wall, and asked Mary to pray with me as I said a *Hail Mary* for everyone who needed prayers.

Before I knew it, that Rosary was finished. It was one of the most powerful experiences of prayer in my life, and I was hooked—*with* Mary—from that moment on. She became my companion in praising Jesus, my personal prayer warrior, and my role model of a grace-filled life. I began relating to Mary and fell in love with her openness to God's Will and receptivity to the Divine Life within her. I started listening to CD's and reading books about Mary, such as Dr. Scott Hahn's *Hail Holy Queen*. Gradually, I came to understand more fully what is meant by *full of grace (Luke 1:28)* and *blessed are you among women. (Luke 1:42)* Belief in her Immaculate Conception, her Assumption, and her crowning as Queen of Heaven were no longer stumbling blocks as I prayed the Rosary every day and continued to read Scripture. *A great sign appeared in the sky, a woman clothed with the sun, with the moon under her feet, and on her head a crown of twelve stars. (Revelation 12:1)* Despised by Satan from the beginning of the world, she is the New Eve, the Ark of the New Covenant, made more glorious than the purest gold, with no stain of sin, *for nothing will be impossible with God. (Luke 1:37)* And so, over time I came to love Mary privately through prayer and study.

The second event occurred July 20, 2005, during a week-long USSSA World Series baseball tournament in Novi, Michigan. Day after day, John, I watched you play numerous games in the sweltering heat, and one day when the coach announced a two-hour practice before game time, I simply could not take it any longer. I needed time away from baseball fields and over-zealous baseball parents. My goal was to find a church or Eucharistic adoration chapel somewhere—anywhere! On the hotel computer, I checked masstimes.org and was overjoyed to find a cloistered Dominican monastery in Farmington Hills. It was only minutes away, and the Eucharistic adoration chapel was open to the public. Alleluia! I dropped you off at the fields and spent the next two hours in glorious silence, solitude, and prayer with Jesus in Eucharistic adoration.

Then, I went to the monastery gift shop. It was here that I confronted Mary. Hanging on the wall was a large tapestry depicting the Blessed Mother holding Jesus in her arms. Her eyes and face were focused downward, on Jesus. I stopped and stared. It was beautiful. I stood motionless for a long time, pondering the message of this tapestry. Repeatedly, I found myself saying, "Keep your eyes on Jesus. Keep your eyes on Jesus." At that moment, I recalled the statue in St. Ferdinand's Eucharistic adoration chapel in which Mary is holding Jesus in the same way—eyes downward, focused on Him. I realized that Mary's beautiful message is so simple, yet powerfully revealed in Scripture and in art: *Let it be done to me according to your word, (Luke 1:38) Do whatever He tells you, (John 2:5)* and "Keep your eyes on Jesus." I loved this message. I wanted to buy the tapestry. However, fear of displaying such a big tapestry of Mary in our home suddenly came over me, and I quickly talked myself out of it. "You are at a baseball tournament. You don't want to carry this around. You have to get on a plane. The metal bar won't fit in your luggage. You can't hang this tapestry up all year long—maybe just at Christmas. What would people think?"

This silly conversation within my brain went on and on, yet there I stood, motionless, staring at the image of the Blessed Mother. I could not walk away. Fortunately, Scripture broke through: *When Jesus saw His Mother and the disciple there whom He loved, He said to His Mother, "Woman, behold your son." Then he said to the disciple, "Behold your Mother." And from that hour, the disciple took her into his home. (John 19:26-27)* The last line resonated in my heart. The disciple took Mary *into his home*. My mind was flooded with questions as I pondered the crucifixion scene, and I had goose bumps from head to toe. "Could I be that disciple? Do I *want* to be the disciple whom Jesus loved? Could I love Jesus enough to bring Mary into *my* home? If I had been standing at the foot of the Cross, would I have refused this final gift of Jesus simply because I didn't want people to think I loved Mary too much? Or, would my love for Jesus have caused me to say 'yes' in an instant, and would I have been *honored* to have Mary in my home?" These were pivotal, crucial questions for me, and the bottom line was this: Did I want Mary in my home for all to see, and would I give her a place of honor? I felt Jesus asking me personally, "Patty, would you take my Mother into your home?" I had a choice to make.

Needless to say, I couldn't refuse Jesus. I bought the tapestry, and from that day on, I brought Mary into our home. Every night before you go up the stairs and every morning as you come down, you see this wall hanging of the Blessed Mother. Every person who enters our front door is welcomed by this image as well because I want Mary's message to permeate our home: "Keep your eyes on Jesus." But most of all, the tapestry reminds me that Mary is our Mother, and I no longer want to keep her hidden. We are all called to be like the disciple John at the foot of the Cross and receive the gift of our spiritual

Mother Mary with honor and love. We are also called to imitate Jesus in all things. So, what did Jesus do in regards to Mary? The Son of God chose to enter her virginal womb, and He physically took on her DNA. He was molded and shaped by Mary. He was fed by her, He learned from her, and He was subject to her for thirty-three years.

We, too, should spiritually enter into Mary, take on her "spiritual DNA," be molded and shaped by her, be spiritually fed by her, learn from her, and be subject to her. In doing so, we are only imitating Jesus Christ. To become like Jesus, we must first be molded by Mary. Theologically, if we think we can "skip" Mary or bypass her, we will only miss out on aspects of Jesus. Think of visiting a newborn baby who has just been brought home from the hospital. Is it even possible to visit the baby without acknowledging or visiting the mother who just gave birth to that child? Can you imagine "oohing" and "ahhing" over the baby, but refusing to say one word to the mother—completely ignoring her? It wouldn't be right because they are so intimately connected.

And that's what I now find so beautiful about Jesus and Mary. They are so intimately connected—at Jesus' birth, at his first miracle, at his Passion, and at his Death. Especially at the foot of the Cross, Our Lady of Sorrows shows us the strength of love in the midst of life's cruelest sufferings. She teaches us how to suffer *with* someone. Though her heart, too, was pierced as she watched her beloved Son being tortured and crucified, she did not refuse the heartache. Mary knows what it is like to lose someone you love—someone who is a part of you. She knows what it is like to feel helpless to "fix it" or solve the problem. She couldn't change the outcome. She couldn't take the place of her Son. She could only stay until the end, just to "be there" in love. Her lessons here are universal—and oh, so relevant to our own lives. As a parent, I can only tell you that I cannot fathom the depth of her sorrow. I fainted when you had wisdom teeth pulled, I cried when you had surgery, and my heart broke whenever you faced rejection of any kind. I have much to learn from Mary's compassionate, maternal heart—from her purity, her humility, and her "yes" to God in all things.

Though I will fail you as a mother many times throughout your life, I take comfort in knowing you have a perfect Mother in Heaven. Love her. Honor her. Become her devoted sons and daughter. Take Mary into your own home and into your heart with Jesus. Remember, your true character is revealed in how well you treat your mother. In everyday, ordinary life this is true of course—but equally true in the spiritual life as well.

I entrust you to the Sacred Heart of Jesus and the Immaculate Heart of Mary, two hearts that beat as one. With confidence in her maternal protection, I pray for your holiness, your purity, and perseverance in faith.

Remember O Most Gracious Virgin Mary, that never was it known that anyone who fled to thy protection, implored thy help, or sought thy intercession was left unaided. Inspired by this confidence, I fly unto thee, O Virgin of virgins, my Mother. To thee do I come, before thee I stand, sinful and sorrowful. O Mother of the Word Incarnate, despise not my petition, but in thy mercy hear and answer me. Amen.

♡ mom

Valentine's Day 2012
Feast of Sts. Cyril and Methodius

Chapter 9

The Pope—and why I want you to obey him

"I announce to you a great joy. Habemus papam. We have a Pope."
(Cardinal Jorge Medina Estevez's proclamation to St. Peter's Square,
April 19, 2005)

Dear John, Julie, and Kevin,

I don't know why, but whenever I see a young father lovingly interact with his children, I get choked up. I can't help it. When I see a dad tenderly holding a newborn baby, walking with his daughter on his shoulders, or kicking a ball with his little boy, I stop and smile. I giggle inside. I watch and remember. I remember precious moments with my father, dancing on his shoes, sledding down the hill on his lap, and building snowmen in the back yard. You, too, have shared many special moments with your dad as he coached your teams, taught you to drive, and helped you with math homework. As toddlers, you loved to walk on his back as he lay on the family room floor, laughing so hard you would eventually fall right on top of him. Julie, you shared your "first date" with your dad at age thirteen, and he has looked forward to dancing with you at every father-daughter banquet for the past four years of high school. These are precious moments to treasure forever.

John and Julie play with Dad

Julie and Dad dance together

Kevin and Dad share a baseball victory

John rides a tricycle with Dad

Your dad has changed jobs twice in his life—both times in order to be home more, travel less, and be a better father. He has protected you, sacrificed for you, and delighted in you more than you will ever know. That's what a good father does for his children. He demonstrates unconditional, strong, self-giving love. He reflects the very love of God. And that is why we desperately need more visible, tangible, Godly fathers in our world today who show us the love of the Heavenly Father. The value of a strong father in the life of a child cannot be underestimated, and the role of fathers to lead their families, to make the tough decisions, and to provide moral guidance is crucial. Simply put, there is no replacement for fatherhood. No matter how our society tries to fill the void, the absence of fathers is catastrophic on every level.

And that is why I love that *"We have a Pope!"* He is the visible, tangible, spiritual Father of our incredible Catholic "family" here on earth. With over one billion brothers and sisters worldwide, we need a leader, we need someone to make the tough decisions, and we need moral guidance here and now. "The Lord made St. Peter the visible foundation of his Church. He entrusted the keys of the Church to him. The Bishop of Rome, successor to St. Peter, is head of the college of bishops, the Vicar of Christ, and Pastor of the Universal Church on earth." (*Catechism of the Catholic Church*, 936)

It is important to note that like St. Peter, our Holy Father is not perfect. Remember, Pope John Paul II went to Confession every week, and Pope Benedict XVI, after first being elected Pope, said these words to the world from the balcony of St. Peter's Basilica:

> "Dear Brothers and Sisters, after the great Pope John Paul II, the cardinals have elected me, a simple, humble worker in the vineyard of the Lord. I am consoled by

the fact that the Lord knows how to work and to act even with inadequate instruments." (Pope Benedict XVI, April 19, 2005)

A few days later at his inaugural Mass, Pope Benedict acknowledged his human weakness again:

"Now, at this moment, weak servant of God that I am, I must assume this enormous task, which truly exceeds all human capacity ... But I am not alone ... Pray for me, that I may not flee for fear of the wolves." (Pope Benedict XVI, April 24, 2005)

No, the Pope is not perfect, but when it comes to matters of faith and morals, the Pope is infallible. As successor to St. Peter, he is guided by the unerring Holy Spirit and commanded by Jesus Christ to preserve and explain the truths of the faith. *Whatever you bind on earth shall be bound in Heaven; and whatever you loose on earth shall be loosed in Heaven. (Matthew 16:19)* For this reason, I place myself under his authority, and I love him as my spiritual Father on earth. He is not some distant ruler, a strict enforcer of laws, nor some harsh old man who relishes power or is out of touch. Rather, our Holy Father is God's chosen, visible shepherd who unites the flock, preserves the faith, teaches us truth, and proclaims Jesus Christ to the world with love. He is the "Servant of Servants" who, like Christ, lays down his life for his sheep.

I have been blessed to see two Popes (so far) in person, and both events stand out as great moments in my lifetime. When Pope John Paul II came to St. Louis in January 1999, your father and I had tickets to the Papal Mass. In order to attend, however, we had to wake up at 2:00 a.m., leave our car at a designated parking lot, and stand for hours in the dark to board shuttle buses. We joined 50,000 fellow Catholics outside the

Trans World Dome in long security lines and waited inside for three more hours before the Mass actually began. It was worth every minute. Your Uncle Tom Hart was one of the banner carriers, and we were so excited to see him be a part of this tremendous, grace-filled, historic event in St. Louis. The Mass was beautiful. It was a joyous occasion, a great day of celebration. We were so happy to be Catholic, so proud of our city, and so grateful to see Pope John Paul II in person—though he was visibly weak and frail. The night before, over 20,000 teens cheered for this man, flocked to see him, sang with him, and prayed with him. He was greeted with "rock-star" excitement and joy by young and old alike, by politicians, the media, and religious leaders of all faiths.

And yet, he unabashedly proclaimed Jesus Christ as the hope for salvation. He boldly defended the family, the Sacrament of Marriage, and the moral teachings of the Church. His message was hardly mainstream or politically correct. He even asked the governor to commute the sentence of a Missouri death-row prisoner to life without parole. The governor complied. For the forty-eight hours that Pope John Paul II was in St. Louis, the winter weather miraculously complied as well with sunshine and record-high temperatures. No one could believe it! This was a true gift for the thousands who stood outside for so long to see him. It was a near perfect two days.

On October 20, 2004, knowing that his Parkinson's disease was progressing and his time on earth would end soon, I wrote Pope John Paul II a letter in which I personally thanked him for being such a gift to the universal Church. I also thanked him for his *Theology of the Body* and explained how much it meant to me. Though it doesn't matter now, I sometimes wonder if he ever read this letter or if someone read it to him. As a saint in Heaven, Pope John Paul II knows how grateful I am. I can't wait to meet him again someday because he is truly one of the greatest heroes of my life. I was thirteen years old when he became Pope, and for nearly twenty-seven years, he spiritually, socially, and morally impacted the modern world like no other individual. He impacted my personal life, my marriage, and my faith like no other as well.

I will never forget the moment on April 2, 2005, when the world paused for John Paul II's death. Kevin, you had just made your First Holy Communion at St. Ferdinand Church, and as soon as Mass was over, the bells began to toll. His funeral was the largest funeral in human history. Over 400,000 mourners packed St. Peter's Square, and millions more watched on television. Although I was grateful that John Paul's suffering had ended and that he had gone home to be with the Lord, I initially felt lost without him because he had been such a good shepherd, a loving spiritual Father to the world, and a living witness to Christ in our midst. I loved him dearly. Now more than ever, I feel incredibly blessed to have lived during his pontificate and to have seen a saint with my own eyes.

Thankfully, the line of succession is never broken! Pope Benedict XVI quickly became a beloved spiritual Father to me as well, and I am grateful that our entire family saw him in person when we visited Rome in 2010. What a gift it was to see the Vatican, to see the Chair of St. Peter, and to visit the tombs of Popes Pius XII, John XXIII, Paul VI, and John Paul II. Most of all, I wanted you to experience for yourself the joy of seeing the Vicar of Christ on earth and to feel that personal connection with the Holy Father. We all witnessed this joy and excitement at the Papal Mass for the Feast of Sts. Peter and Paul. We stood on chairs to get a better glimpse of Pope Benedict and snapped pictures with the crowds. We all heard parts of the Mass in different languages from around the world, yet we felt right at home in St. Peter's Basilica with the Holy Father, Cardinal Burke, and bishops from near and far. We sang and celebrated with complete strangers, but sensed we were with our own Catholic "family." I hope you never forget that moment. Also, whoever the Pope may be at any given time in the future, I hope you feel that the Pope is *your* Holy Father. Place yourself under his authority and the Magisterium of the Church—out of love and humble obedience to the successor of St. Peter.

In the early Church, there was no doubt that Peter had primacy. It was Peter who proposed that a replacement should be chosen for Judas; it was Peter who gave the speech at Pentecost. Peter spoke before the Sanhedrin, presided over the Council of Jerusalem, and settled early arguments in the Church. Peter performed miracles of healing and raised Tabitha from the dead as well. People *even carried the sick out into the streets and laid them on cots and mats so that when Peter came by, at least his shadow might fall on one or another of them. (Acts 5:15)* They wanted to be in the presence of Peter's shadow! Why? Because they recognized him as the Vicar of Christ on earth, plain and simple.

When we join the crowds to see the Pope, when we yell, "*Viva il Papa!*" or wave flags in joyful celebration, we are no different than the early Christians wanting to see Peter. We are simply recognizing his primacy. The Pope is not Jesus; he is not God. However, he is the successor of Peter, the visible Pastor of the universal Church and spiritual Father of us all—and that is reason enough to rejoice.

In today's culture, it is not easy to be in union with the Holy Father and defend the office of Pope. Many want to choose their own morality, form their own conscience of personal preference, and promote majority rule in the Church. They refuse to obey a "celibate old man in Rome." This is how dissent from the Church and disunity often begins—by ignoring the teachings of our Holy Fathers. If you have questions or doubts about the Church's teachings, I encourage you to read the Catechism and Papal encyclicals for yourself. For years, I thought Papal writings would be way too difficult, too theological, and completely over my head. Therefore, I never bothered. I didn't care what the Pope taught on issues of our day. I was wrong. Now, as I read more and more encyclicals from various Popes, I find myself saying, "Genius! How prophetic. This is *truth*. Thank God for his courage."

I often wonder how many Popes I will live to see. I wonder what the future will bring for your lifetime and if we will witness the election of the first American Pope. Who knows? It could happen. For now, I trust the Holy Spirit to guide the Church. I pray for the Holy Father every day and pray that all Christians will be united someday under his authority. May you obey him, respect him, and defend him. Like a good father, he will protect you from error when it comes to matters of faith and morals.

Habemus papam. YES! We have a Pope. You can count on it until the end of time.

Mom

February 27, 2012
Feast of St. Gabriel Possenti

Chapter 10

The Saints—and why I want you to imitate them

"Oh, oobe doo, I wanna be like you. I wanna walk like you, talk like you, too ..."
("I Wanna Be Like You" from Walt Disney's "The Jungle Book")

Dear John, Julie, and Kevin,

When I was a young girl, I wanted to be like Julie Andrews. I had seen *The Sound of Music* dozens of times and could imitate every word from every song in my perfected British accent. By the time I was eighteen, I had short blonde hair, had played the leading role of *Maria von Trapp* in a community theater production, and had gone off to Europe to be a nanny myself. I was living my dream. The first time I went hiking in the Alps, I couldn't resist finding a secluded meadow, and with arms open wide, I twirled around in a circle and burst out singing, "*The hills are alive, with the sound of music!*"

But I'm not the only one who has ever had silly dreams of being someone else. My sister Peggy wanted to be like Peggy Fleming. My dad wanted to be like Harry "*The Cat*" Brecheen. When I asked him, "Who in the heck is Harry '*The Cat*' Brecheen?" he immediately responded, "You don't know Harry Brecheen? He pitched for the St. Louis Cardinals, won three games in the 1944 World Series against the Browns, and shares the same birthday with me on October 14th. I can tell you *everything* about Harry '*The Cat*' Brecheen! They used to call me '*The Cat*' because I wanted to be just like him!" What a riot. I had no clue who the man was, but to my father, Harry Brecheen was a revered soul mate from his childhood.

You, too, have had your share of childhood heroes. At some time or another, your bedrooms became shrines to baseball players, Super Bowl champions, World Cup soccer greats, or Hollywood teen stars. Though you may be embarrassed now at the thought of all your old posters, they were a part of your dreams—a part of growing up. As parents, we tried to ensure that you knew a variety of role models, not just popular athletes or entertainers, but inspiring leaders in history, art, and science as well. That is why we took you to so many museums and monuments. I smile at the thought of standing in line to see the Lombardi Trophy when it was on display in St. Louis, walking through *Graceland* in Memphis, gawking at Michael Phelps' swimming goggles in Baltimore, and staring at the First Ladies' Inaugural gowns at the Smithsonian Institute. We have also seen the *Mona Lisa*, Michelangelo's *David*, Mount Rushmore, the Vietnam War Memorial, and countless other world-class monuments that recognize excellence and heroism.

Our nation, along with every other culture, builds statues to commemorate a person's contribution to society; we display precious artifacts in museums to remember our stories of struggle and triumph; we have national holidays to celebrate George Washington, Abraham Lincoln, and Dr. Martin Luther King, Jr. For every human endeavor, we have a Hall of Fame filled with memorabilia of its heroes as well. Why do we do all this? Because we are naturally drawn to excellence. We want to remember, preserve, and commemorate greatness. We seek heroes.

And that is why I love the saints. They are my heroes—and more! The saints show us how to love Jesus with a total, radical, unconditional "yes." Their lives give witness to the universal call to holiness in all circumstances, for every state of life, throughout the entire history of Christianity. They remind us of our ultimate destiny, Heaven. Unfortunately, we often regard sainthood as some lofty, unattainable goal that is possible only for a few pious individuals who do nothing but sit around and pray all day long. Not true. Saints are real, ordinary people who lived daring lives for God. Some of the greatest people who have ever lived are officially canonized, and they constitute the Church's "Hall of Fame," but all who enter into Heaven are also considered saints, and that is the goal for all of us. Sainthood is for you and me, and the first step in becoming a saint is actually quite simple: Desire it.

This hit me like a ton of bricks on October 2, 2004, when we saw the movie *Thérèse*. While the screen was still dark, we heard the child-like voice of St. Thérèse begin with these words: "I want to be a saint." Instantly, I had goose bumps from head to toe. I had never heard anyone in my world actually say these words so plainly, directly, and yet so beautifully. She desired sainthood. She articulated and visualized it. For Thérèse, her proclamation sounded as natural as saying, "I want to be a teacher," and in that moment, I realized that the saint dares to dream *bigger*. A saint trusts that with God's infinite mercy, *all* things are possible—even sainthood.

I want you to know that I desire to be a saint with all my being. My goal for you is to be a saint as well—because the alternative is nothing short of hell. There is no "in between." Either you become a saint in Heaven, or you will live for all eternity in hell. So then, have you ever thought of sainthood? Can you picture yourself as a saint? Have you dared to dream of being a *great* saint? Were you to become an artist, you would study Da Vinci, Rubens, and Monet. If your dream were to be a great golfer, you would be familiar with Jack Nicklaus, Arnold Palmer, and Tiger Woods. And if you are serious about following Christ, then you should know the saints as your personal mentors. Look to "the Masters" and discover some amazing new (and old!) heroes. Be inspired by their greatness and holiness. It could change your life, as it did mine.

My journey with the saints began in earnest when I discovered St. Catherine of Siena on her feast day, April 29, 2003. Catherine's life, enthusiasm, and boldness in speaking about the unity of the Church inspired me. She was feminine, yet displayed an unusual drive and energy. She liked flowers and loved to sing as she moved about. When I read these personal details of her life, I remember thinking, "I can relate to this woman. We have something in common." Just knowing she had an optimistic outlook on life and loved to sing gave me my first real connection with a saint. Two years later when I was asked to speak at a priests' deanery meeting, it was St. Catherine of Siena who inspired me to say "yes," despite my fears of incompetence and unworthiness—for if God could choose an uneducated woman who could neither read nor write to give council to bishops, cardinals, and Popes during the Middle Ages, then He could certainly choose an ordinary housewife like myself to give one small talk to a group of local priests.

As I struggled with self-doubt during my early years of public ministry, it was St. John Chrysostom who became my spiritual soul mate and helped me to realize I was born to do this. On my 38th birthday, I went to chapel and read the daily Mass readings as well as a reflection for the saint of the day. For the first time, I discovered that I was born on the feast of St. John Chrysostom. I had never heard of him. I couldn't even pronounce his name. But when I learned that Chrysostom means "golden mouth" and that he is the patron saint of preachers and speakers, I almost fell over in the pew. I wrote in my journal:

> "St. John Chrysostom, intercede for me and become my patron saint. As I begin to speak more and more, may my mouth become "golden" and bring glory to God. May I speak of love, mercy, forgiveness, compassion, kindness, and truth. Guide me to be the witness Christ has called me to be ... I guess when all is said and done, I was born on the feast of St. John Chrysostom—a person who was given a big mouth (just like me!) God turned it into a "golden mouth" and made him a saint. Wow! That's a lot to live up to. Lord, I want to be "golden" too. Help me desire it with all my heart. Mold me. Shape me—and my mouth, too. Make me holy.

> This is one of the most special birthdays of my life. The gift of this saint will be with me now forever. Thank you, God. It's like finding out who I am, and who I am called to be in *your* eyes. I can't help but wonder: God, did you choose my birth date from all eternity? DID YOU KNOW I'D HAVE A BIG MOUTH? Did you know when I was born that I would love to talk? Of course you did, and I am in awe of your plans for me. Your timing, your Word, and your calling are UNBELIEVABLE. Your gift today is too much for me

to even comprehend. THANK YOU, GOD." (Journal entry: September 13, 2003)

Every time I discover a new saint, I am initially drawn to what we have in common. I feel as if I have found a long-lost relative. In a certain sense, I have. In the family of God, the saints are our great-great grandparents, aunts, uncles, and cousins. We *are* "related," and we do have more in common than we realize. Often, we share just tiny coincidences. For example, St. Teresa Benedicta of the Cross (Edith Stein) was extremely busy and often exhausted as a young professor and lecturer; St. Gianna was an ordinary wife and mother. I can relate!

What truly connects us with the saints, however, is our common faith. We receive the same Eucharist at Mass. We pray before the same Blessed Sacrament. We sing the same ancient hymns and read the same Gospels. St. Rose Philippine Duchesne, known as the "woman who prays always," lived and worked just five minutes from our home here in Florissant, Missouri. We are literally walking in her footsteps every day as we go about our business. How amazing that God raised up a great saint from our parish!

And just as we have old portraits of your great-great grandparents hanging upstairs, we also have books and pictures of the saints in our home because I want you to know your ancestors in faith. Know your roots. Be encouraged by their stories, strengthened by their legacy, and feel their presence as they walk with you on your journey. *Therefore, since we are surrounded by so great a cloud of witnesses, let us rid ourselves of every burden and sin that clings to us and persevere in running the race that lies before us while keeping our eyes fixed on Jesus, the leader and perfecter of faith. For the sake of the joy that lay before Him He endured the Cross, despising its shame, and has taken His seat at the right of the throne of God. Consider how He endured such opposition from sinners, in order that you may not grow weary and lose heart. (Hebrews 12:1-3)*

The more I read about the lives of the saints, the more I am consoled in knowing their faults as well. St. Jerome had anger issues. St. Teresa of Avila was proud as a teenager and talked too much in her youth. St. Dominic Savio got in trouble at school for outbursts of laughter. St. Dismas was a convicted felon. St. Margaret of Cortona was the mistress of a nobleman and had a child out of wedlock. St. Catherine of Genoa and her unfaithful husband went bankrupt. She was lonely and depressed. St. Joseph of Cupertino was considered quite dumb by all who knew him, even his own mother. Their list of faults goes on and on, but that is what makes them real and gives me hope. If St. Thérèse of Lisieux could admit that she sometimes fell asleep during prayer, then there is hope for me! The saints are proof that God's grace is far greater than any sin, for He continues to choose incredibly flawed individuals to carry out His mission. The saints also prove that anyone—at any age—can have a true conversion of heart.

My reality check comes, however, when I read about their sufferings. For years, my sister and I have secretly desired to be Sts. Perpetua and Felicity. Peggy often jokes, "You be Perpetua, and I'll be Felicity." Whenever we sing the Litany of the Saints, we smile at the chanting of their names because our dream is to replace it with "Sts. Peggy and Patty, pray for us!" Then, we quickly remember that their martyrdom in the year 202 was anything but a joke. Perpetua was a young wife and mother, just twenty-two years old. Felicity was married and expecting a child. Three days after Felicity delivered her baby, they were both flogged, lead into the amphitheater of Carthage, and beheaded before cheering crowds. Some in their group were killed by wild leopards. Many saints throughout history suffered similar cruelties: St. Bartholomew was flayed alive and then beheaded; St. Maximus the Confessor had his tongue cut out; St. Lawrence was roasted on a gridiron; and St. Maximilian Kolbe suffered for weeks in the starvation bunker at Auschwitz. He was ultimately injected with carbolic acid to hasten his death.

I can only marvel at their courage and perseverance. What would I have done? Could you or I ever have that kind of strength? How did they endure such pain and torture, yet remain steadfast in faith? How did some, like the Martyrs of Compiègne, remain joyful in the midst of evil? How could they sing the *Salve Regina,* the *Te Deum,* and the *Laudate Dominum* as they were carted off to execution during the French Revolution? These are sobering but necessary thoughts to ponder, especially in light of our secular society where Catholic faith and morals are increasingly met with outright hatred. With story after story, the saints give witness to the power of love over evil. They demonstrate that heroic virtue not only exists, but is possible when we focus on prayer, Heaven, and the Passion of our Lord Jesus Christ. They teach us to say "yes" in the thousand small sacrifices of ordinary life, so that our final "yes" will simply be a natural continuation of intimate union with Christ. We need the example of the saints now more than ever to stay strong, defend the faith, and persevere in difficult times.

Finally, the saints are powerful prayer warriors who intercede on our behalf. They are more fully alive in Heaven than we can fathom, and their prayers rise up like incense before the throne of God: *If then, we have died with Christ, we believe that we shall also live with Him. (Romans 6:8) Each one had a harp and they were holding golden bowls full of incense, which are the prayers of the saints. (Revelation 5:8)* What a gift! If only the world knew! We have a multitude of ancestors and "friends in high places" who pray for us—just for the asking.

I thought about the intercession of the saints in October 2010 when the world rejoiced at the safe rescue of thirty-three

Chilean miners who had been trapped sixty-nine days underground. Every media outlet around the globe covered this miraculous story, and millions were glued to their TV as one by one, these men were slowly brought to the surface. I stayed up late and cried tears of joy as they hugged their families and thanked God to be alive. What many news broadcasters didn't report, however, was that the rescue mission was called *Operation San Lorenzo*. You see, one of the first things the Chilean miners requested when they were initially trapped was a crucifix and a statue of St. Lawrence to be lowered into the shaft. St. Lawrence is the patron saint of miners. They also asked the people to pray for his intercession and to parade the statue of St. Lawrence throughout the town. A large statue of St. Lawrence, complete with a lamp and miner's hat, was brought to the site of the collapse. The town held parades and prayer vigils with St. Lawrence as their intercessor. Their prayers were answered, and by the grace of God, this story had an unbelievably happy ending.

But I wonder ... if a mine had collapsed here in America, would we have thought to ask the Blessed Mother, St. Joseph, St. Lawrence, and all the saints to pray? Would we have even known that St. Lawrence is the patron saint of miners? Would we have paraded through our streets in prayer, holding statues and candles, begging God for the safe rescue of our men? I doubt it. Yet, if you believe in the power of prayer, then you naturally want as many people praying for you as possible in any crisis. Often, we "get the word out" to family and friends with urgent prayer requests. We ask those who are faithful, holy, and close to God to seriously pray. Typically, you wouldn't ask an atheist to pray for you, right? Who better than the saints, who are closest to Jesus, to pray for us! Don't forget to ask the best prayer warriors in all of history—your ancestors in the faith who are alive in Christ.

Chapter 11

Prayer—and why I want you to crave it

"Until you are convinced that prayer is the best use of your time, you will never make time for prayer."
(Anonymous)

Dear John, Julie, and Kevin,

This summer, your father and I will celebrate twenty-four years of marriage. Our relationship has grown so beautifully over the years since I first met him at age fourteen on my first day of high school. Who would have thought that the guy sitting behind me in geometry class would be my future husband? Certainly not I! For the next seven years, your father wasn't even on my radar. Sure, I liked your dad in high school. He was nice, polite, smart, and admired by many. Being on the honors track, we had almost every class together and knew many of the same friends. Once, when I was sixteen, he took me to see *Raiders of the Lost Ark,* but that was it. I did *not* want to date your dad—and told him so on numerous occasions. I never gave him much thought. He was just Larry Schneier—always there, always nice, always polite—a friend, but nothing more. In college, I was searching for "Prince Charming" to sweep me off my feet, and my plan was to live happily ever after in Europe. But as we matured into our early 20's, my eyes were finally opened to your father's integrity, honesty, and kindness. I suddenly saw Larry Schneier in a whole new light, and I wanted to know more about this man who had been with me all the while. We started spending every free moment together, and soon our friendship was transformed into love. My search was over.

Now, after twenty-four years of marriage, I still love being the wife of Larry Schneier. He is my best friend, the love of my life, my confidant, and soul mate. Your dad and I enjoy so many ordinary things in the midst of our hectic schedules— like cooking, taking walks, holding hands, and eating lunch together. It may seem silly, but thirty minutes together at the kitchen table during his lunch break is a tremendous gift for our relationship. We connect. We are present to each other. We talk about everyday "stuff" and simply enjoy each other's company. Your father could go out to lunch every day at a restaurant if he wanted; he could stay at the office and eat with his co-workers, too. Instead, he chooses to come home almost every work day, eat a sandwich, and spend those thirty minutes with me. I am the luckiest woman in the world to be his wife.

Little things—like sitting together on the couch, doing dishes, and giving back rubs—matter in a marriage. Time spent doing "nothing" is important as well. Sometimes, words are not even necessary. Your father and I can walk on a beach and stare at a sunset in complete silence, for example, yet feel extremely close. What matters is that we are together, that we appreciate each other, and that we connect on a daily basis. We both crave one-on-one time alone, just the two of us. Within marriage, this is not an option. It's a necessity. I long to be in his arms at night, whisper our inside jokes, giggle together, and celebrate life's joys. In times of sorrow, I share my tears. If I only talked to my husband when I needed something, if I didn't thank him for all the things he does for our family, if I only gave him five minutes of my time when we are on the go or two minutes before my head hit the pillow at night, our relationship would be *awful*. Our love would be cold, one-sided, and stagnate. It would quickly die.

And so it is with God.

I've known God all my life. He has always been with me. But I never dreamed of more or desired more until I began a life of committed, quiet, reflective, meditative prayer. Sure, I knew the standard Catholic vocal prayers, and I went to church every Sunday to pray. I also prayed before meals and in times of need. I thought I prayed enough. I was content with this friendship and simply wanted to keep the status quo. In my early days of mothering when I was exhausted at every moment, I certainly didn't think I had time to fit quiet, reflective, meditative prayer into my busy schedule. You kids were my first priority, your dad was second, and my personal prayer life was a distant third. I had my priorities completely backwards. "The interior life, like love, is destined to grow. If you say 'enough' you are already dead." (St. Augustine)

Now I realize that in order to love rightly and become the wife and mother I want to be, I must first go to the source of love itself and be filled with God's love. Otherwise, I am running on empty and spinning my wheels. I have also learned that nurturing love takes time, and time will always be my most precious commodity—with any relationship or any endeavor.

Every morning I face the same question regarding time: Should I start my to-do list or spend time with my Creator, the Lover of my soul? The busier I am, the more I actually need prayer, and the more I fall in love with God, the more I desire it. I crave one-on-one time with God, carefree time doing "nothing" together, or time just thanking and praising Him. I need time to simply connect, to converse and listen to His whispers within my heart. Sometimes, no words are spoken. Other times, my tears won't stop. But no matter what happens during that sacred time together, it is always the *best* use of my time. Prayer is not an option for the spiritual life. It's a necessity. Without daily prayer, my relationship with God would become cold, one-sided, and stagnate. My spiritual life would quickly die.

The first and most important step in developing an interior life of prayer is to commit to a specific time and place— and then show up. This is absolutely crucial. For example, in order to get to know your father, I obviously showed up for our dates. Likewise, in my lifelong desire to stay physically fit, I must commit and show up for my morning workout. Some mornings, I may not feel like getting out of bed at 5:30 a.m., but knowing that my neighbor Cheryl is waiting for me in her basement, I get up and go anyway. I arrive half asleep. Sure enough, within minutes I am running on the treadmill, talking with Cheryl, sweating like crazy, and feeling wide awake. I come alive and feel strong! We have enjoyed working out together for years, and we have seen the long-term benefits. If I just show up, the rest takes care of itself.

The same is true with prayer, day in and day out over the course of many years. It doesn't matter how I feel *before* I begin my prayer time because my emotions could be happy or sad, frustrated or excited. What matters is that I simply come before the Lord. God takes care of the rest. He awakens my soul, and I come alive! The long-term benefits are worth every minute in His presence.

> "Lord, I'll be honest. I didn't want to come here this morning. It was a battle of wills. But how can I *not* thank you that my children got to school safely in this ice? How can I not thank you that we have a warm house when it is -7 outside? How can I not thank you that Larry has a job in this recession? And now that I'm here before you, I'm glad I came. My to-do list is inconsequential—meaningless in your presence. It doesn't matter. You give perspective; you relieve stress. You let me know there is nothing to fear, nothing to stress over. I surrender it all." (Journal entry: December 16, 2008)

My favorite place of prayer, which has actually become my favorite place in the whole world, is the perpetual Eucharistic adoration chapel at St. Ferdinand Parish. And just as Cheryl is waiting for me to work out in her basement, Jesus Himself is physically present, waiting for me in chapel 24-7, 365 days a year for prayer. Day or night, He humbly waits under the appearance of bread so that I might behold Him. Here I experience beautiful silence and solitude before the Lord; here I can truly focus on God and leave everything else behind. "We need to find God, and He cannot be found in noise and restlessness. God is the friend of silence." (Blessed Teresa of Calcutta) In my busy, crazy, noisy world, I yearn for this silence, sitting face to face with God and just *being*. One gaze at the monstrance, and I am quieted. My soul is at rest.

> "The gift of this chapel—of perfect solitude in your presence, Lord, is so powerful! It's just you and I! I come before you, my Creator, my Father, my Redeemer, the Lover of my soul, my Friend, and I am safe in your

arms, secure in your loving embrace, comforted by your presence and your mercy. There is nothing to hide; you know every thought, word, and deed. You know my inmost being—the good, the bad, the ugly—and yet, you love me anyway. You fill me. I stretch out my hands with an empty cup, and you overflow it! If I come to you angry or frustrated, you take it and replace it with peace. If I bring you sin, you take it and give me forgiveness. If I bring you worries or weaknesses, you take them and give me strength. Solitude! Beautiful solitude! I feel like Adam before God, experiencing original solitude and perfect happiness in the garden. I feel that here in this chapel before you, God, face to face in this beautiful silence." (Journal entry: January 8, 2008)

If only the world knew the peace that could be theirs! If only Catholics understood this foretaste of Heaven! If only everyone knew of the transformation that occurs just by sitting before the Real Presence of the Lord. When I sit face to face with all Truth, Beauty, and Love, I cannot hold on to bitterness, resentment, grudges, pride, or disobedience. They begin to melt away. Jesus begins to chisel my hardened heart with gentle inspirations, encouragements, and loving thoughts that infuse my being. I am overwhelmed by His mercy and love as I sit at His feet. I am on holy ground in the presence of my Creator, filled with gratitude and joy. What a way to start the day! I have a date every morning at a specific time and a very special place. The God of the Universe, who loves me from all eternity, is waiting for me—and I can't get enough of His love. Our one-on-one prayer time together is the fuel that keeps this fire within me burning.

The hardest part of my day is leaving my glimpse of Heaven and switching to earth, where I must hit the ground running. Yet, prayer doesn't end simply because I walk out the doors of chapel. God is with me at every second, wherever I go. The key is to remain in His presence all day long, to converse with Him as I go about my work, and remember that I am never alone. At home or in the car, running to the grocery store or to the bank, waiting in an airport or doctor's office—all of these have become places of prayer. My entire day is an opportunity to pray for others, and my favorite way to do this is by reflecting on the events in Jesus' life through the Mysteries of the Rosary.

My life has never been the same since discovering the Rosary in 2002 and falling in love with it in 2003. I love the Rosary because it is physical *and* spiritual, structured yet spontaneous. While I hold each bead and move through the Rosary, the words and rhythm of the *Hail Mary* become my "background music" as I ponder the Mysteries and pray for special intentions. Without the Rosary, I would not seriously pray for all the people I love or for those who are suffering. I would forget. But now, when I say to someone, "I'll pray for you," I mean it—physically and concretely. With just one Rosary, I am praying for fifty intentions, one for each bead. All day long, often on my ten little fingers, I pray. I specifically pray for you during my Rosary as well: the first bead is for your holiness; the next is for your purity; one bead is for your health. I continue praying for your safety, your future vocation, your studies, and your friends as I move through the body of the Rosary.

> "I can't stop saying *Hail Mary's* for the whole world all day long. My mind is reminded of anything and everything, and I begin praying for the person in front of me, for the person behind me, for the people in the stores, the airport, etc. I pray Rosary after Rosary for virtues, for my family, for the Church, for the world, for all who are suffering. I'm praying for the prisoner,

the prostitute, the priest, the Pope, the politician, the pilot, the policeman. One letter of the alphabet or one word will set my mind in motion. I can't stop. Everyone needs prayers. Thank you, God, that I can talk to you anytime, anywhere. Thank you, that no prayer is ever wasted or goes unheard." (Journal entry: March 14, 2008)

The benefits of prayer are revealed to me most powerfully when "life happens." Do you remember when I had a flat tire on the way to one of your baseball games, and I sat by the road for an hour, waiting for a tow truck? That turned out to be a beautiful hour of prayer. Do you all remember when I was stranded in the Chicago airport overnight and couldn't get home? I found the airport chapel and spent most of the night there. It was awesome. John, do you remember the time when you were hours late at the golf course, and I was waiting to pick you up, calling and calling on your cell phone to no avail? Had I not said the Rosary in the car, I would have yelled at you and made a scene that day—guaranteed. Kevin, do you know what I was doing during every soccer game when a certain parent screamed from the sidelines the entire time? I was praying the Rosary. Julie, do you remember the summer before high school when I had to drive you forty-five minutes each way for math and volleyball camps? Do you know what I did during those hours of waiting? I found a Eucharistic chapel nearby and spent quality time with God in order to keep my sanity.

Time and time again, when the weight of the world gets to me—when I am crushed, hurt, stressed, worried, disappointed, afraid, or simply exhausted—I run to the Lord in prayer. He never disappoints. Other times, I am so filled with joy, I can't wait to sing His praises and thank Him for His goodness. I bring it all to Him: the good, the bad, the highs, and lows. I am no expert, and there are a million different ways to pray, but I hope you will seek an intimate prayer life with your Creator, who is the fulfillment of all your desires. He is waiting for you every day to just stop by and see Him. Schedule some one-on-one time at your favorite quiet place and show up. I know you are busy. That's all the more reason to begin now. Start with ten minutes a day. It is the *best* possible use of your time—I promise. Soon, you may discover that you can't get enough of His love, and you'll want more. May you thirst for silence, hunger for solitude, and crave time with God in prayer. Your spiritual life depends on it!

♡ Mom

March 19, 2012
Feast of St. Joseph, Patron of the Interior Life

Chapter 12

The Sanctity of Life—and why I want you to defend it

"Before I formed you in the womb I knew you, before you were born, I dedicated you."
(Jeremiah 1:5)

Dear John, Julie, and Kevin,

I was seven years old when the Supreme Court decision in *Roe v. Wade* legalized abortion in this country. I remember seeing brochures on the dining room table and asking my mother what they were. I'm sure she didn't want my innocence destroyed that day by seeing graphic photos of aborted babies, but it was too late. I had noticed them under a stack of newspapers, and I wanted to know. That was the day I first learned about abortion. I'll never forget it because my mom was

129

pregnant at the time with my brother Mike, and she explained that she could now legally choose to kill the baby inside her. As a seven year old, I didn't fully understand, but I knew it was wrong, and I was horrified by those pictures. Within that year, the first pro-life rallies were organized in St. Louis to protest the Supreme Court decision, and I remember our family marching downtown along with thousands of people, church leaders, and politicians. I remember complaining about being tired and not wanting to walk five miles. I just wanted to go home. But march we did—with my new baby brother in a stroller—and I learned a valuable lesson that day: It didn't matter that I was tired. Some things were more important.

That lesson would come back to haunt me thirty years later. In the meantime, my life moved on. I grew up, focused on my studies, taught high school, married, and became your mother. Like most adults, I became "busy" and absorbed with my own responsibilities. I also became complacent to the fact that over 53 million babies had been destroyed by legalized abortion and that a holocaust was taking place every day in hospitals and clinics in my own back yard. For many years, the extent of my involvement was to vote for pro-life candidates and sign a paper rose once a year at church, urging our politicians to vote for pro-life legislation. That was it. And yet, I wanted *you* to be pro-life as you grew older, and I wanted *you* to care about the unborn, the elderly, and the disabled. Soon, I could no longer remain passive as I watched our culture slide further down the slippery slope of death in areas of abortion, euthanasia, and embryonic stem cell research. I found myself asking, "What have I done to stop this evil? If I don't stand up, who will? What is my excuse? How can I teach my children the importance of these life issues?" It no longer mattered that I was too busy or tired, that I had to travel a long distance and stand out in the cold, or that I hated politics. Some things were more important.

And so, when you reached the age of twelve, I took each of you on a special trip to the National March for Life in Washington, D.C. You received a lesson in democracy and freedom; you became a voice for the most defenseless and vulnerable; you saw for yourself this beautiful pro-life movement that has defended the inalienable right to life for all members of society and has persevered since 1973. Do you remember the thousands of joyful young people who packed into the streets, singing and praying? Do you remember the courageous women who shared their testimonies and held signs saying, "I regret my abortion?" Do you remember the rally on the Mall with political and religious leaders from all faiths? I hope that these images are forever etched into your heart and that these trips were only the beginning of your own efforts to build a culture of life.

John's first Pro-Life March

It was Bishop Paul Zipfel from the Diocese of Bismarck, North Dakota, who challenged me to go beyond my comfort zone and beyond an annual pro-life bus trip. I was privileged to hear him speak in October 2007, and I will never forget his homily. He told the true story of a woman recounting her early childhood experiences in Germany during World War II. As a young German girl, she attended church every Sunday with her family. This church was located near the train tracks. During services, they often heard screams coming from the crowded train cars. Whenever the trains passed by, the choir and congregation simply sang louder so that they couldn't hear the screams of the Jewish children. Bishop Zipfel went on to say that "we are that choir. We let the busyness of life, the rhetoric of 'choice,' and the desire for political correctness drown out the voices of the unborn. We allow the mass murder of innocent life so long as it is neat and clean, neutralized and impersonal. We mask our language and call it a 'procedure' so as not to sound grotesque. We are living in a time of holocaust."

Because of my personal experiences in Germany, the word *holocaust* evokes much emotion within me. I love the German people, the land, the language, and the culture. I always will. However, I have been to the concentration camp at Dachau on numerous occasions, and the death of six million Jews still hangs over the air. I often think of the Germans and the horror they experienced when they discovered the truth after the war. I've seen video footage of German citizens viewing the concentration camps that were in their own neighborhoods. They stood in utter shock, sobbing over what took place there. They fainted and vomited. These were everyday, ordinary, good people—yet they bore a part of the guilt.

Obvious questions remain: How could they *not* know what was going on? Why didn't they do more to prevent these atrocities? What should they have done? How could a government systematically kill millions of people with so little resistance? These questions resonate in my heart and challenge me when I think of abortion—today, right now, in our country. If we know what is going on inside our local Planned Parenthood and do nothing, we are no different than that "choir" or the masses of people who looked the other way during World War II. As difficult as it is for me to tell you this, I must, for you are old enough to take a stand. You are also old enough to make a difference and to be accountable for your part in this chapter of history.

Don't be misled by those who will claim there are other issues that are equally as important. Nothing comes close.

Abortion is the single most important moral question of our time, the single most divisive issue of our nation, and the #1 destroyer of human life. The magnitude of 53 million lives lost to abortion trumps every other social justice issue. Unfortunately, I didn't always believe this, and I'm embarrassed to admit that I wrote a major paper for a political science class during my college years in which I defended the legality of *Roe v. Wade*. I maintained in my thesis that I was personally opposed to abortion. However, I argued that others had the right to choose based on the constitution. I was "Pontius Pilate"— personally opposed, but just following the law.

When my dad heard about my thesis, a heated debate ensued. I told him it didn't matter if a political candidate were pro-life or not. I insisted that abortion was not the most important issue—that jobs, the economy, and helping the poor were equally as important. I remember his answer: "That's what many people in Germany thought when Hitler came to power in 1933. Don't ever forget, Hitler was great for the economy. He put people back to work, he re-built infrastructure, he brought back national pride, and he was a dynamic speaker. He had charisma, strength, and a vision for a great Germany. He wanted to make medical breakthroughs. There was just this one tiny problem—he didn't value the sanctity of every human being." When you are tempted to consider other issues or tempted to endorse a pro-choice candidate, remember these words of wisdom from your grandfather and know that *life* is more important.

Also, be consistent and defend the right to life of *all* people in all circumstances. That means you recognize the man on death row as a child of God with human dignity and value, even if his life is spent behind bars, even if he never repents. Defend the right to life for that guy, too. Christ died for him. The love of God can penetrate his heart. The criminal on death row is someone's son, someone's brother, a nephew, or grandson. I realize that you may think a mass murderer or terrorist deserves to die. You may not understand how anyone can love a person who commits evil or how God could love that person, but we don't always see things the way God sees. *"For my thoughts are not your thoughts, nor are your ways my ways," says the Lord. "As high as the Heavens are above the earth, so high are my ways above your ways and my thoughts above your thoughts."* (Isaiah 55:8-10)

Pope John Paul II personally showed the world the dignity of every human life—whether innocent or not—when he visited Mehmet Ali Agca, the man who attempted to assassinate him on May 13, 1981, in St. Peter's Square. Inside a prison cell two years later, Pope John Paul II talked with this man and forgave him. He is one of my pro-life heroes because he so beautifully defended and loved every person as a child of God.

Many other pro-life witnesses like Gianna Jessen, Abby Johnson, and the family of Terri Schiavo have heroically shown the world the value of human life as well—often being thrust into the public spotlight at great personal sacrifice. Then, there are the countless unsung heroes who pour out their lives every day with unconditional love: adoptive parents, foster parents, volunteers who work in crisis pregnancy centers, pro-life doctors and nurses, those who care for the elderly and disabled. We are blessed to know many of these heroes. Our lives are enriched because of their "yes" and commitment to life! Just think of all the children we know and deeply love who have been adopted. Yet, for every Tommy, David, Sasha, Anya, John Paul, Josiah, Ethan, Faith, and Mary, there are millions who didn't make it, and my heart weeps.

Every year in late September, I weep for one child in particular, whom I will always remember. In the fall of 2006, my sister called one day to ask if I would pray for a certain woman who was planning to abort her six-week-old baby that weekend. I dropped everything, went straight to chapel, and begged God, "Do whatever it takes to save this baby." I remember desperately praying, "God, give this woman a flat tire on Saturday—or give her the flu—if that's what it takes to make her stay home on Saturday. Do whatever it takes to give her more time so that she will change her mind!" Then this thought stirred from deep within. "What if it takes ... you?" I wrote in my journal:

> "What if it takes Larry and me to save this baby? What if no one else would try to save her baby or tell her that they would adopt her baby, love her baby, and raise her baby in a wonderful family? What if she aborts this child without knowing that? What if this baby is meant to be our baby? So many questions ... only one answer ... I say 'yes,' my Lord. Thy Will be done. What will Larry think? It is not easy being married to me. I know this. How many women come home from chapel and ask their husbands to adopt a stranger's baby? And yet, I know he would say 'yes,' too, in order to save this baby's life." (Journal entry: September 27, 2006)

Your father and I stayed up late that night, talking about the reality of this possibility and what it would mean for us. Then we prayed together, and we both said "yes." The following morning, I called Peggy and told her to get word to the mother that we would adopt her baby. We were serious.

> "Will she accept our offer, Lord? It is not up to us, but up to her now. Is this tiny new life meant to be our child?—only if it is your Will, Lord. I will trust in your plan for our family. This is the biggest decision Larry and I have made in a long time ... a scary decision ... a WONDERFUL decision. Lord, I pray for the mother tonight. SHE has the most difficult decision of her life. I have already become emotionally attached to this

baby. I beg you, Lord, don't allow this abortion. Let us love this child. Let life be victorious! I pray for life! And Lord, thank you for Larry, who is the greatest husband in the world." (Journal entry: September 27, 2006)

Knowing it was a long shot, I tried in vain the rest of the week not to think about the future. Within days, however, I had already chosen names, pictured us as older parents, and giggled at the thought of going to Disney World again. I prayed like never before and was a nervous wreck on Saturday. The following week, we learned the gut-wrenching news that she had aborted her baby. I could barely scribble these words—and nothing more—as I grieved:

"Words cannot express my heartache. The sorrow is real and intense as I ponder the murder of what 'could have been'—our child." (Journal entry: October 3, 2006)

My heart aches for the women and their babies. My heart aches for the fathers. My heart aches for the doctors, the staff, and the volunteers at every abortion clinic in the world, who are good people and believe they are helping women in need. That's why I will fast and pray for an end to abortion. That's why I will stand out in front of Planned Parenthood in the rain or snow, holding a sign and praying for everyone who enters. That's why I will go to our state and nation's capital to defend the right to life and speak all over this country to high school students about real love and the gift of life. That's why I will do anything to help doctors stop prescribing abortifacient contraceptives and convert their practice to NFP-only. God has called me to do whatever I can to build a culture of life. I may only be one drop of water against a tsunami of death, but I will gladly be that one drop of water, and I hope you will, too.

I see sparks in each of you, and I want you to know that I am proud of your pro-life witness in this world. John, your enthusiasm every year in going to the March for Life is contagious. I love that about you. Julie, you have no idea what a difference you make in the lives of your friends, just by recommending that they go see the pro-life movie, *October Baby*, for example. You are evangelizing without even realizing it. Kevin, I joked about you going Christmas caroling with your buddies this past December, but when you boys gave all the collected money to Birthright, I was speechless. What an awesome, beautiful thing to do.

Keep it up. Fight the good fight. With love and compassion, defend the dignity of every person from conception until natural death. I pray you will be stirred into action and persevere in the battle for life. The world needs you!

Mom

Holy Week 2012

Chapter 13

Your Vocation—and why I want you to live it to the full

"Man cannot fully find himself except through the sincere gift of himself."
(Gaudium et Spes 24)

Dear John, Julie, and Kevin,

On the day of your birth, I remember looking in awe at your tiny fingers and ten tiny toes. As I snuggled and kissed your precious little cheeks, I couldn't fathom that one day you would grow up to be the person you are today. Overwhelmed by the thought of all the possibilities that awaited you, I whispered in my heart, "Lord, what are your plans for this child? What will he become? How will she make her mark in this world?" The answers to these questions are a hidden mystery on the day of your birth, to be revealed ever so slowly as you grow and develop.

Of course, your father and I have made many decisions for you along the way and have guided you in developing your gifts and talents. We chose your schools, enrolled you in extracurricular activities, instilled morals and discipline, and raised you in the Church. Now, it is your turn to make the most important decisions for yourself. We get to watch and wait—and be here for support—as you choose your path in this world and discover God's beautiful plan for your life. *"For I know the plans I have for you," says the Lord, "plans for welfare and not for evil, to give you a future and a hope." (Jeremiah 29:11)* This is such an exciting time for you, and I am so grateful to have a front row seat as this mystery unfolds!

Like any mother, I want you to be happy. However, I want a much deeper happiness and joy for you than the culture's standard recipe which calls for good grades, a college degree, a successful career, money in the bank, a house, a car, good health, and maybe a family. Don't get me wrong. All of these are good things, and the pressure to "have it all" is real. But your ultimate fulfillment and happiness will be found in your unique vocation—*not* in your career, your health, or your wealth.

God has chosen you from all eternity to love and to bring life to the world through a particular vocation. You will find the meaning and purpose of your existence when you pour out the gift of yourself in marriage, in the priesthood/religious life, or in the single life through the service of God and humanity. *You did not choose me, but I chose you to go and bear fruit—fruit that will last. (John 15:16)* Thus, the most important questions for you to discern are: *How* am I called to love? *Which* fruit—physical or spiritual—does God want me to bear? *Where* is God inviting me to give the gift of myself? Only God knows these answers for you. Only you can discover them for yourself through intimate conversations with Him in prayer, but your time of discernment has begun, and this process is so crucial for your future happiness that you must discern carefully. The story of the rich young man from Mark's Gospel demonstrates why:

The young man asked Jesus, *"Good Teacher, what must I do to inherit eternal life?"* And after Jesus explained the Commandments to him, he replied, *"Teacher, all of these I have observed from my youth."* *Jesus, looking at him, loved him and said to him. "You are lacking in one thing. Go, sell what you have, and give to the poor and you will have treasure in Heaven; then come, follow me."* *At that statement his face fell, and he went away sad, for he had many possessions. (Mark 10:17-22)* Jesus certainly didn't tell every single person He met to sell their goods, give to the poor, and follow Him. But He did ask this young man to do so—out of love. Jesus was telling the young man his personal vocation, his unique pathway to inherit eternal life.

Unfortunately, this young man didn't accept the invitation. He missed his vocation and all its joys because he had other plans for his life. *And he went away sad.* How tragic! In a similar way, your vocation is like *a treasure buried in a field, which a person finds and hides again, and out of joy goes and sells all that he has and buys that field,* or like a merchant searching for fine pearls. *When he finds a pearl of great price, he goes and sells all that he has and buys it. (Matthew 13:44-45)* Once you find this treasure or pearl, no other earthly goods can compare. Life is changed from that moment on.

I almost missed countless joys in my vocation as wife and mother because of other plans, and I had to gradually learn what it means to "sell all that I have" in order to gain real treasure. Throughout my childhood, I dreamed of becoming a teacher. I studied abroad, graduated *summa cum laude*, and miraculously landed the job of my dreams at age twenty-two, teaching English and German in one of the most prestigious private schools in the Midwest. Many of my students came from families who drove Porsches and BMWs. They attended presidential inaugural balls and made newspaper headlines in sports, medicine, or business. They were generous, wonderful families, who welcomed me with open arms into their world of fancy parties, extravagant gifts, and influential connections.

At the same time, I poured myself out twelve hours a day for my students. I tutored those who needed help, coached cheerleading, organized community service projects, and attended school events. I loved teaching, and I was good at it. For four years, I didn't think anything could fulfill me as much as teaching. Then I became a mother, and nothing could prepare me for the fulfillment—as well as the challenges—that awaited me as your mother.

To my surprise, the deepest desires of my heart changed. I wanted to pour myself out for love of *you*, and I was no longer happy in what was previously "the greatest job ever." I tried for one entire school year to balance both teaching and motherhood, but despite a reduced teaching load, I was miserable. The perks didn't matter anymore. Coaching, preparing lesson plans, and grading papers every night became a burden.

Out of love, God was inviting me to embrace my vocation as wife and mother full-time, but like the Apostles, I had some "nets" that I first needed to drop. *At once they left their nets and followed Him. (Matthew 4:20)* Did this require sacrifice? You bet. Every vocation requires sacrifice. Was it worth it? Absolutely. But contrary to what you might think, I did *not* give up my dreams, my gifts, or my talents. You were *not* a detour to my success. No. All my dreams, gifts, and talents have been fulfilled as wife and mother—far beyond what I could have possibly imagined.

Obviously, God doesn't call every wife and mother to quit her day job. He doesn't call every religious sister to teach in a school, every priest to run a parish, or every single person to work in ministry either. Each vocation is unique and personal. However, once you discern your vocation, remain faithful and make it your priority over work, leisure, and any other commitments. Your vocation is meant to point you to Heaven and become your pathway to holiness, love, joy, and fulfillment. Discovering your personal vocation is one of the most important moments of your life, and when lived with enthusiasm, your vocation will be a source of happiness and peace even in times of suffering. On the other hand, if you distort your vocation, betray your vocation, or miss it all together, life can become a living hell of brokenness, bitterness, resentment, and isolation—no matter how much money is in the bank or how successful you might be in your career.

I can only speak from experience in regards to marriage, but I must say that I love being married to your father. I was made to love him freely, faithfully, totally, and fruitfully. Likewise, your father was made to be a gift for me and love me in good times and in bad, in sickness and in health, 'til death do us part. The joy we experience in living this out as husband and wife is indescribable. It's a glimpse of

Our Wedding Day, July 22, 1988

Heaven. Truly, we are head-over-heels in love with an unquenchable fire that will last forever. You can count on that.

However, our love will last forever, not because we happen to be one of the "lucky ones," but rather by the grace of God and the power of His Redemption to transform our hearts. We have had our share of arguments and misunderstandings. We have sinfully wounded and disappointed each other as well. At times, it seems as if a wedge is lodged between us, and we will never see eye to eye due to our opposite temperaments. Ours is an imperfect, fallen marriage to be sure, and that glimpse of Heaven can be clouded on any given day for a number of selfish reasons.

Precisely in these times, we remind each other of our marriage slogan: "As a team, we are unbeatable." He begins the statement, and I finish it. Unity is always our goal, always our priority, and we will do whatever it takes to restore unity—even if it means staying up all night. Believe it or not, we have learned how to argue in whispers so as not to wake you. Sometimes we are still talking and crying until the wee hours of the morning. But we always persevere until we are one again in mind, body, and spirit—until we can forgive each other, hold each other, pray together, and recognize the gift of each other again.

Last summer, I needed to be reminded of this unity. Chaos erupted over what should have been a very special weekend for just the two of us, and I was livid with your father and extremely hurt by his lack of planning and initiative. This is the real, ordinary, messy stuff of marriage, recorded in my journal as I wept in chapel. Looking back, it seems ridiculous that I could get so mad over one weekend, but at the time, I was crushed:

> "When my tears won't stop, there's only one thing to do: Run to you, O Lord, and let it all out. And so today I come to cry and to pray for the perspective, wisdom,

and the grace to forgive and forget. How can I be so hurt and so disappointed by my husband, who I know loves me? He just blew it, that's all, and it shouldn't be such a big deal to me, but it is. I feel miles apart from my husband. Nice job, Satan. You certainly put a wedge between us—and I made it all too easy for you. I let you in.

How can we turn this whole mess around? How can I first just stop crying? Lord, I know I am equally to blame. I should have communicated to Larry my ideas for the weekend. I know better than to hold on to resentment. I can't expect him to read my mind. I'm sorry I blew it. I'm sorry, Lord. Take my tears, Jesus. This is silly of me. I know in my head this is no big deal—it's just the difference between men and women manifesting itself. After twenty-three years of marriage, this is just one minor disappointment, which cannot even compare to the life of love, joy, and countless beautiful memories we have shared. I must focus on that truth. I love him, and he loves me. That will never change. We just express it differently sometimes.

Our source of love is you, Lord. You have ordained our marriage from all eternity and blessed us abundantly. Your love and the love we have for each other are so much greater, so much more powerful, than Satan or our own sinfulness. Love is always victorious over sin. Forgiveness unleashes love. Our love will prevail this weekend—not my tears. I resolve to focus on our love. I resolve to make the most of what time we have on Saturday and NOT see the glass ½ empty or "what could have been." I resolve to enjoy whatever we end up doing, not to mope, complain, or feel sorry for myself. Lord, give me a spirit of gratitude for my husband. Give me the perspective to see beauty all around me. Restore the joy. Turn off the tears.

Thanks for being here today. Thanks for letting me sit at your feet and just cry. Thanks that you love me even when I whine and act foolish, with false expectations and easily hurt feelings. Jesus, thanks for understanding my heart. Thank you for my precious Larry and the gift of our marriage. Redeem us. Reconcile our hearts. Unite us again in love. Sanctify and bless this whole weekend. Amen." (Journal entry: July 15, 2011)

On this occasion, as in many others, my tears were literally turned into joy through the power of forgiveness. Our memorable weekend was spent biking through vineyards in the country, taking walks, and making our own special candlelight dinners together. But none of that would have happened had we not reconciled. No doubt, forgiveness is one of the things I love most about our marriage and family life. The mercy and love of Christ transforms us and sets us free to love and forgive. And so, yes, we are fallen, but we are also redeemed, and we choose to live in that joy of Redemption every day and to rediscover the truths of married love. We still have much to learn, but we rejoice in knowing that we get to spend the rest of our lives loving, forgiving, sharing, dancing, giggling, praying, celebrating, and parenting together. Marriage is our way—our lifelong journey—to live out our vocation to love. Oh, how I love this glorious plan of God!

Likewise, our family is blessed to know many holy, faithful, joyful priests and religious sisters, who gloriously give witness to a spiritual marriage and spousal communion with Christ and His Church. They bear great spiritual fruit! You have seen the beauty of their vocation lived out in the details of everyday life and the sacramental life of the Church. They freely give of themselves out of love for us as their spiritual children, and their joy is contagious. They, too, are in love, and it shows!

John, as you continue to study at the seminary and discern your vocation to the priesthood, I am filled with gratitude for your "yes" to God, for listening to His voice within your heart, and for being open to this awesome vocation to love. You have already taken the first step: *Come, and you will see. (John 1:39)* Now, as in any relationship, you must wait patiently and see how this invitation to love develops, how it blossoms, and how it matures. No matter what the future holds, know that I will always be proud of you for entering the seminary and for seriously discerning your vocation. If this is your calling, you have my complete, unconditional support—for ever since you played "Holy Thursday" as a four year old and "consecrated" your lunch at the kitchen table, I have pondered this possibility in my heart.

Julie and Kevin, the same is true for you as well. If you discern God calling you to the religious life, go for it! If God chooses you for the single life, embrace it with joy and live it to the full. You have so many gifts and talents that can be used in the service of God and humanity. Pour yourself out for the good of others, and in doing so, you will bring life to the world and find fulfillment. If you are called to marriage, make it a holy marriage. Put God at the center of your relationship and pray with your spouse. Your love will be all the richer when it is rooted in God's love.

How can you best prepare yourself to give and receive this awesome love found in your vocation? How can you best prepare to receive the deepest desires of your heart? Chastity. "Only the chaste man and the chaste woman are capable of love." (Pope John Paul II) Chastity is essential at any age, whether you are eighteen or eighty years old. It is essential for every vocation, too, whether you are called to be celibate for the Kingdom, married, or single. The best decision your father and I ever made as young adults was to remain chaste before marriage, and it was the greatest wedding gift we could have possibly given to each other. To this day, he still says to me, "I am so glad you are the only woman I have ever loved."

Our biggest mistake, however, was assuming that chastity was only for teens and that once we were married, it was no longer necessary. We lost the purity to recognize counterfeits to love and allowed these counterfeits to creep into our bedroom. We lost the vision of God's design for total union and communion within marriage, and we fell for the lies of the world. In re-discovering chastity through the *Theology of the Body*, we have re-discovered our capacity to love and the awesomeness of every vocation. You owe it to yourself and to your future marriage—whether physical or spiritual—to immerse yourself into the *Theology of the Body* and discover the meaning of love, life, and chastity as it relates to your own unique vocation.

Finally, I just want you to know that you don't have to have everything figured out yet. In fact, it's impossible. Be open to wherever God leads you and be patient. You may discover your vocation early in life; you may find it much later. That's okay. You will know you have discovered it when you can say from the depth of your being, "I was made for this! I was born to love like this!" In the meantime, develop your gifts, talents, and virtues. Listen to the whispers and deepest desires of your heart in prayer. When you do discern your unique vocation, trust that God will give you every grace to remain faithful, to persevere, and to live it out with joy!

I pray this vocational prayer every day for you because I love you so much.

God our Father, bless your Church with an abundance of priests, deacons, brothers, and sisters. Give those you have called to marriage and those you have chosen to live as single persons in the world the special graces that their lives need. Form all of us into the likeness of your Son so that in Him, with Him and through Him, we may love you more deeply and serve you more faithfully. And Father, help me to know and to live my vocation. With Mary I ask this through Jesus, our Lord. Amen.

Mom

May 1, 2012
Feast of St. Joseph, the Worker

Chapter 14

The Cross—and why I hope you will embrace it

"I consider that the sufferings of this present time are as nothing compared with the glory to be revealed for us."
(Romans 8:18)

Dear John, Julie, and Kevin,

This is the hardest letter for me to write, and so I've saved it for last.

As I look at each of you, standing at the threshold of your future, about to embark on your own pathways, I am overwhelmed with happiness and hope. John, next year you will complete your undergraduate degree. Julie, in just a few short months you will head off to college and leave home for the first time. Kevin, you are gaining new independence as you learn to

151

drive and earn a paycheck at your first job. Life is good. You have worked hard in school and made good choices. Nothing stands in the way of your dreams or the opportunities that await you. You are richly blessed with a loving family, a good home, health, and everything you need. Most importantly, you are grateful for it all and recognize the countless blessings that God has given you. The same could be said for your father and me. Life is good. Our health, our home, our family, and everything we have are gifts from God. We can't thank Him enough. Our praise can only scratch the surface of our grateful hearts.

Julie's high school graduation, May 2012

But what if everything were stripped away? What if we were hit by a devastating tornado like the one in Joplin or an earthquake like the one in Haiti? What if one of us were diagnosed with Lou Gehrig's disease or a brain tumor? What if our family became a victim of random violence or experienced war in our own streets? What if one of us were in a tragic accident that left us physically or mentally impaired for the rest of our lives? What if a member of our family were abused or violated? What then? How would we respond? You see, it is easy to enjoy faith in good times. It is easy for us to give back, to sing *How Great Thou Art* and *Awesome God*, and know that He is good. But none of us have truly experienced long-term suffering, loss, hunger, poverty, war, genocide, or a debilitating illness.

When I think about these things, I start asking, "Why, God? Why do you allow so many to suffer? Why them and not me? Why can I walk, talk, and eat so easily, when right now at this moment, someone I love will never walk or talk or eat real food again? Why is life so unfair for children born in poverty and children living with cancer? Why are so many women I know widows at such a young age? ... And when will it be my turn to suffer? What tragedies await us? What trials will my children have to endure in the future?" These are the questions that rock me to the core and cause me to struggle as I try to comprehend the mystery of suffering.

When I was your age, I used to believe the motto: "You choose your own life." Now, I realize that no one chooses suffering, and so much of life is beyond our control. No parent chooses to lose a teenage son or daughter to suicide. No one chooses to be hit by a drunk driver. No one chooses to be blind or deaf. The older I get, the more I see how much of life is actually imposed upon us by others, by the forces of nature, by circumstances, or by illness.

And yet, despite what is done *to* us or the circumstances beyond our control that dictate our future, we will always have one crucial decision in the midst of any pain or suffering: How will I respond to it? We have two choices—to draw closer to God or turn away from Him. Our answer determines our outlook on life, our perception of God, and our ultimate identity. Suffering *will* transform us. It *will* change us, whether we like it or not. The question is *how*? Our response to suffering will either make us or break us. *Whoever does not take up his Cross and follow after me is not worthy of me. Whoever finds his life will lose it, and whoever loses his life for my sake will find it. (Matthew 10:38-39)*

True story: Once there was a boy who lived in a small town. His mother died when he was just eight years old. Three years later, his brother died of scarlet fever. He grew up with his father, graduated from high school, and went to work. Shortly before his 21st birthday, tragedy struck again. His father died of a sudden heart attack, and he was left completely alone with no immediate family. When World War II broke out, he lost many close friends. Some were rounded up in concentration camps, and he never saw them again. He narrowly escaped death numerous times in his lifetime. Once, he was shot. Years later, he was diagnosed with Parkinson's disease. He suffered greatly from this debilitating disease and eventually died.

How tragic ... or so it would seem, had these not been the minor details of Pope John Paul II's amazing, joyful, grace-filled life. Did suffering impact him? Of course it did. But he chose to be transformed into the image of Christ, to unite his suffering with Christ on the Cross, and to trust in God's awesome plan for his life. "There is a way of living the Cross with bitterness and sadness, but it breaks our spirit. There is also the way of carrying the Cross as Christ did, and then we perceive clearly that it leads to glory." (Pope John Paul II, *Spiritual Advice from Pope John Paul II*) This is the secret to suffering—to embrace the Cross.

Think of people we know and love who have endured great suffering. Some encounter tragedy after tragedy, and their lives are miserable. The mention of their name brings sadness to our hearts. It's depressing. However, we know others who have also experienced long-term suffering, yet our response is totally different when we think of their life. Just say the name Chris Zandstra or Claire Murphy in our family, and we don't think of cancer or death. We don't get depressed at all. We think of supernatural faith, overwhelming joy, inspiration, strength, love, and tons of laughter. We can't help but smile in awe and admiration. Trained in the school of suffering, they prove it is possible to carry the Cross with joy, unending hope, and even glory—just like the saints.

Though I can't shield you from the storms of life that are sure to come, I pray you will "suffer well" and draw closer to Christ. When I went through many medical tests, a bone marrow biopsy, and major surgery, my friend Dr. Michael Dixon taught me the secret to "suffering well." He said, "You have just been given a 'gift card' to be used on behalf of those you love. Don't waste it." In other words, I had just been given an opportunity to participate with Christ in the work of Redemption.

And so, during every difficult procedure, I offered my pain for those who were far worse off and in need of prayer. (Let's face it—no matter what we are enduring, there is always someone else who is suffering more.) I prayed for every person I knew who had cancer, for those who were in need of a job, or for those who had lost a loved one. This took the focus off of me and lessened the pain. Rosary after Rosary, I concentrated on the *Agony in the Garden*, the *Scourging at the Pillar*, the *Crowning with Thorns*, the *Carrying of the Cross*, and the *Crucifixion*. I must have repeated "Thy Will be done" a hundred times as I surrendered my life into God's hands. I wrote in my journal:

> "Thank you, Lord, for being with me during the bone marrow biopsy. Prayers for women in prison, for all mothers facing an unexpected pregnancy, and for all who have cancer made it bearable. What would I do without the rhythm of the *Hail Marys* and my ten fingers? Thank you that it's over. Now I wait for the results. I offer up the waiting, too, for those who are waiting for their loved one to come home from Iraq or Afghanistan, or for those who are waiting to find a job. Thy Will be done in me, Lord. I give you my bone

marrow and every test they will run. Do with it as you like. This road of medical tests may only be the beginning. Thy Will be done. I want whatever you want, Jesus. I want whatever will bring me closer to you." (Journal entry: July 10, 2008)

This is the only way I know how to get through the trials of life—praying, surrendering to God's Will, and offering pain for the benefit of others in union with Christ. It sounds silly, but I simply picture myself climbing up on the Cross. Admittedly, my trials have been small, but I am grateful for every tiny "gift card" God has granted me to be offered for those I love. St. Francis de Sales summed it up beautifully:

"Learn to embrace your crosses. Be assured that God's Will for you is both just and merciful. Recognize suffering as a sign of God's love. If we look at trials apart from God's Will, they are bitter. If we consider them in that eternal good pleasure, we find them all gold, and more lovely and precious than can be described."

In a few weeks, I'm scheduled for Mohs surgery again. I'll be praying for you the whole time. Someday—perhaps sooner than later—when I experience long-term suffering, severe pain, or loss, please remind me of these truths. Don't let me waste it.

Finally, no matter what life may throw at you, no matter how difficult your circumstances may seem, or how long your sufferings may last, do not lose hope. Suffering never has the final word for those who hope in Christ Jesus. Remember, Easter always follows Good Friday. God is with you at every moment with His Holy Spirit to strengthen, comfort, and sustain you. Cling to Him in your darkest hour. Cry out in your agony. Give Him your fears, your doubts, your tears, and your pain. Then, surround yourself with truth and remind yourself repeatedly what you know about God: He loves you. His Will is perfect. He will never abandon you. He makes all things new, and He heals the brokenhearted. His Kingdom lasts forever, where every tear will be wiped away and there will be no more suffering! This is your destiny and your hope.

My favorite song about hope is *Beauty Will Rise* by five-time-Grammy-winning songwriter Steven Curtis Chapman. I blast this song in my car! At home I dance in the family room, pump my fists to the rhythm, and sing along at the top of my lungs. It's such an upbeat song, and yet the lyrics move me to tears when I recall the Chapman family's life-changing tragedy on May 21, 2008: Steven Curtis Chapman and his family were just hours away from celebrating their oldest daughter Emily's engagement and their son Caleb's high school graduation, when their five-year-old adopted daughter, Maria, was accidently hit and killed in the driveway of their Franklin, Tennessee, home. The driver of the SUV was Maria's older teenage brother, Will. In the midst of his personal grief, this famous Christian singer and songwriter became a witness to the world, writing an entire album about faith, hope, and love that are born of suffering. *Beauty Will Rise* powerfully declares that the hope of Heaven triumphs over our deepest sorrows.

> *It was the day the world went wrong/ I screamed 'til my voice was gone/ And watched through the tears as everything came crashing down/ Slowly panic turns to pain/ As we awake to what remains/ And sift through the ashes that are left behind/ But buried deep beneath/ all our broken dreams we have this hope/ **Out of these ashes/ Beauty will rise/ And we will dance among the ruins/ We will see it with our own eyes/ Out of these ashes/ Beauty will rise/ For we know joy is coming***

in the morning/ In the morning/ Beauty will rise/ So take another breath for now/ And let the tears come washing down/ And if you can't believe, I will believe for you/ 'Cause I have seen the signs of Spring/ Just watch and see/ Chorus/ I can hear it in the distance/ And it's not too far away/ It's the music and the laughter/ Of a wedding and a feast/ I can almost feel the hand of God/ reaching for my face to wipe the tears away/ And say it's time to make everything new/ Make it all new/ This is our hope/ This is the promise/ This is our hope/ This is the promise/ It will take our breath away/ To see the beauty that's been made/ Out of the ashes, out of the ashes/ It will take our breath away/ To see the beauty that He's made out of the ashes, out of the ashes/ Out of these ashes/ Beauty will rise/ And we will dance among the ruins/ We will see it with our own eyes/ Out of this darkness/ New light will shine/ And we'll know the joy that's coming in the morning/ In the morning/ Beauty will rise/ Beauty will rise

"Beauty Will Rise" from the album *Beauty Will Rise,* words and music by Steven Curtis Chapman. Copyright © 2009 Sparrow Records

Thankfully, this story doesn't end with just a song. In 2009, Steven Curtis Chapman and his family traveled to China near the ruins from the devastating 2008 earthquake to do a concert for the survivors and share the hope that sustained them. They also opened a brand-new, beautiful special-needs orphan facility in China in honor of their daughter and named it *Maria's Big House of Hope.* Steven's wife, Mary Beth, has written a book called *Choosing to See: A Journey of Struggle and Hope.* They recently became proud grandparents of a baby girl.

Time and time again, fruit is born of suffering, and God does create beauty out of ashes. So when life disappoints you, or your dreams come crashing down, look all around and choose to see hope. It is visible in the blossoming flowers and budding trees. It is written in the Word of God and found deep within your own heart. God is weaving a beautiful tapestry of your life. Let Him choose every thread, every color, and every design. In the end, it will be far more glorious than you could have ever imagined, full of the richness that includes both joys and sorrows.

Embrace it all!

Mom

May 27, 2012
Feast of Pentecost

Acknowledgments

I could not have written this book without the unwavering support of my husband, Larry. He is my living, breathing "St. Joseph" and the love of my life. How blessed I am to be his wife and experience a glimpse of Heaven with him at my side. Truly, this was a team project, and I relied on his expertise and advice.

I am grateful to Peggy Hart, Katie Brennan, and Sr. Raffaella Cavallin who encouraged me to write and provided crucial feedback from start to finish. They shared in the vision for this book. Also, thanks to Mary Hilmes, Teresa Holman, Duff Foshage, Katie Robinson, and Dan Hart for their help with details.

Finally, my deepest gratitude goes to John, Julie, and Kevin who have taught me so much about God's love through the joys (and struggles) of parenthood. I thank them for allowing me to share these letters with the world. May God be glorified.